James

Book I: Chapter 1

Volume 22
of
Heavenly Citizens
in Earthly Shoes

An Exposition of the Scriptures for Disciples and Young Christians

Randy Green

© 2021 Randy Green

ISBN:

ISBN-13: 9798594533288

Dedication

This book is dedicated to Mr. Mark Green. Our Heavenly Father and His blessed and only Son Messiah Jesus saw fit to birth us into the same family. By His matchless grace, He has also rebirthed us into His eternal Family. We haven't been able to spend much time together here in time and space. We will make up for it in eternity. I look forward to being with you there, brother. The name of our blessed Lord and Savior Jesus Christ be praised!

Heavenly Citizens

Earthly Shoes

Acknowledgments

Scripture quotations taken from the New American Standard Bible®, Copyright © 1960, 1962, 1963, 1968, 1971, 1972, 1973, 1975, 1977, 1995 by The Lockman Foundation. Used by permission. (www.Lockman.org)

Author's Note

Rather than use quotation marks, I will as a rule *italicize* Biblical quotations of chapter/verse. I will also follow such a format when quoting other sources. I will use **bold type** and italics for key words and phrases. I will use <u>underline</u> or *italics* for purposes of emphasizing certain words and phrases.

Table of Contents

Dedication 2

Acknowledgments.. 3

Author's Note 4

Table of Contents 5

Forward 6

Introduction 10

   A. Why Start This Blog? - Part One 10

   B. Why Start This Blog? - Part Two....................................... 12

   C. How, And How Not, To Study The Bible........................... 18

The Book of James: An Introduction – Part 1 27

The Book of James: An Introduction – Part 2 35

James 1:1 (Part 1)... 43

James 1:1 (Part 2)... 53

James 1:1-3 63

James 1:3-5 73

James 1:5-6 83

James 1:6-9 93

James 1:9-12 103

James 1:12.. 113

James 1:12-13 123

James 1:13-15 133

James 1:15-16 143

James 1:16-18 153

James 1:18-19 163

James 1:19-21 173

James 1:21-22 183

James 1:22-25 193

James 1:25... 203

James 1:26-27 211

Forward

The Scriptural exposition which comprises this book was written between August 2020 and January 2021. The reader may find it advantageous to read other writings on my websites:

- https://bibleprophet.wordpress.com/
- http://bibleprophet-koe.blogspot.com/

Here is the description of the second website's purpose, as stated at the top of the site:

> *Jesus insisted, "You must be born again" [John 3:3]. Liberal Christians won't go there; evangelical Christians stop there: Jesus starts there! A baby is BORN crying, being spoon-fed and having his diaper changed; but he cannot continue like that throughout his life! At some point this baby grows to a toddler...a boy...a youth...a man. A Christian is one who is BORN AGAIN. So why in even "good" churches do newborns not grow into Biblical manhood? My website explores this issue.*

Being a series of daily entries as they are, the individual articles find cohesion through continuous repetition—which is to say, I begin each article by recalling where I ended the previous article. This provides not only cohesion but also **context**.

The idea of such repetition is not original. It is in the Bible, when Moses instructed the Israelites how to raise their families (cf., Deuteronomy 6:1-12). And consider Peter's teaching technique:

> *So I will always remind you of these things, even though you know them and are firmly established in the truth you now have. I think it is right to refresh your memory as*

long as I live in the tent of this body, because I know that I will soon put it aside, as our Lord Jesus Christ has made clear to me. And I will make every effort to see that after my departure you will always be able to remember these things [2 Peter 1:12-15].

This book is not written with the seminary student in mind. It is for the Christian who has yet to embark upon his or her journey through the Bible and wants to begin now. It is for the young Christian—not "young" in the sense of how many years he or she has lived, but "young" in the sense of how much he or she has studied the Word of God and thereby grown in the grace and knowledge of our Lord and Savior Jesus Christ.

Whether a Christian is 18 years old or 80 makes no difference. If you desire to know who God is and what He wants with your life, and then respond affirmatively to what He teaches you, you have come to the right place! Read on, dear Christian, read on.

Even though I have not written with the seminary student in mind but with the young child of God as the disciple, nonetheless I have not written at an elementary school level either. This book is not suitable for elementary school children or even middle school kids. However, some high school young adults will benefit from it, so let them not be deterred from the trek.

I have tried to present the *Books of Titus & Philemon* in such a way that the reader might not only sip on some milk but also chew on some meat. The two together make for a healthy meal.

My book won't be digested through a cursory browsing with minimal exertion, as is the case with many of our modern Sunday School lessons and sermonettes. By definition a disciple is someone who wants to learn and grow spiritually, so as to go forth in his walk with the Lord. This requires effort and commitment. No pain, no gain.

To make this more palatable, I decided at the initial outset of the *Heavenly Citizens* series that I would follow the format I originally used, viz., daily articles which were displayed on my blog. Many Christians enjoy using a daily devotional booklet for their quiet time with God. Such booklets provide a brief article of two or three paragraphs, based on a short Scripture reading for each day. In this way the Christian can be instructed about a Biblical thought and goaded into meditating on the thought.

The shortcoming of such daily devotionals is that they provide only milk, which in and of itself will not nourish a growing child. It suffices for the newborn, but continued feeding on only milk cannot help but make for malnourished saints. I fear that our churches are comprised predominantly of such dear souls. The Lord needs to spur on these good people to discipleship, to spiritual maturity through daily feedings on the whole counsel of God.

I hope I am providing for this need by means of my series *Heavenly Citizens In Earthly Shoes*. It certainly is my intention. The reader is encouraged to read in his or her Bible the specific Scripture text for that article; then to read the article and weigh the teaching by actual chapter/verse; and finally, to finish each study by rereading the text in the Bible once more.

The Bible text will be one verse, two verses, a few verses…seldom more than one paragraph in length, so the reader will not spend a great deal of time reading it. The disciple should be able to read and digest the daily article in about twenty minutes time. If we allow for extra time to reread the Bible text, most any spiritually young Christian should be able to accomplish the feat of reading both the Bible text and the article within thirty minutes a day.

Now this is certainly not requiring much time commitment, considering the reader has made a decision to go beyond spiritual infancy and become a true disciple of Christ. Discipleship is a lifetime commitment, a process of growing more and more in Christlikeness from the point of making a commitment to discipleship until the moment when Christ calls us home. Keeping this in mind, the disciple should want to study his or her Bible from now until eternity. If you do so, you can continue to read the growing volumes of my Bible exposition from now until whenever.

There are 20 articles in this book. By reading an article only five times a week you will complete *James Book I* in 4 weeks (20 articles divided by 5 days per week). This is the equivalent of just 1 month, not long for getting a pretty good handle on what God is teaching us by means of *James 1*. So get to work, dear saint. Don't be fainthearted or indolent. Rather, press on with your decision to grow in your relationship with the Lord.

But please, start off as any responsible disciple should, viz., by counting the cost and resolutely determining to pay that cost. This is what our Lord Jesus taught in Luke 14:28-33:

> *Suppose one of you wants to build a tower. Will he not first sit down and estimate the cost to see if he has enough money to complete it? For if he lays the foundation and is not able to finish it, everyone who sees it will ridicule him, saying, "This fellow began to build and was not able to finish." Or suppose a king is about to go to war against another king. Will he not first sit down and consider whether he is able with ten thousand men to oppose the one coming against him with twenty thousand? If he is not able, he will send a delegation while the other is still a long way off and will ask for terms of peace. In the same way, any of you who does not give up everything he has cannot be my disciple.*

Introduction
A. Why Start This Blog? - Part One

reetings, friends! Welcome to my book series, *Heavenly Citizens in Earthly Shoes*. Let's get to the issue at hand: why write this series?

I have pastored several churches in several different denominations over the course of twenty years. My pastoral experience in these various denominations (rather than in just one denomination) has expanded my intellectual and spiritual horizons, by revealing to me via firsthand experience the different ways Christians of various persuasions think and function vis-à-vis the Bible and its teachings. This perforce has enhanced my understanding of these same Biblical teachings, and of the manifold ways they are applied in the churches and in the lives of Christians individually.

Additionally, I have a Master of Divinity degree (M-Div) from Trinity Evangelical Divinity School (TEDS) in Bannockburn, Illinois. I am also ordained as a pastor-teacher. Now it is a trademark of my educational institution (TEDS) that, for different evangelical positions on Biblical issues, the debating points are explained in the classroom—although the students are not left to themselves to drift along in indecision. Students are required to choose what they believe and defend it academically, while simultaneously analyzing the other evangelical positions and exposing what they deem to be the deficiencies behind them.

This method generates pastors and teachers who think through the Bible and learn to analyze doctrines on the basis of God's Word— what Paul refers to as "the whole counsel of God" (Acts 20:27)— as contrasted with picking out a verse here and another verse there to "prove" my points. So instead of having been taught the "party line" (which makes for good parrots), I was encouraged to read the

Bible and prayerfully think. Plus knowing the different ways Christians through the centuries have viewed these issues only helps me to consider more of the facts. After all, partial truth is not truth at all but a distortion of the truth, and this can easily mislead us.

Here's the point to all these words. My background academically allows me to understand the different positions which evangelicals hold, regarding various Biblical doctrines and practices. My background experientially provides me with "live" practical training in this same understanding. And all of this together adds up to a broader recognition of the overall state of contemporary Christianity and the evangelical churches in the USA.

This book will be one installment in my teaching the Bible from Genesis 1:1 all the way through Revelation 22:21, chapter by chapter and in **context**. But more on this in Part Two of the *Introduction*.

B. Why Start This Blog? - Part Two

In our last study I made a concerted effort at two things. First, I stated what I consider to be the paramount problem in the Christian community today, viz., either ignoring the Bible altogether (the liberals) or else picking and choosing a few favorite elementary doctrines while ignoring the remainder of the Bible (the evangelicals). Secondly, I presented my credentials for why I am qualified to diagnose this problem and to prescribe the cure. Today I will endeavor to offer my analysis and then prescribe the cure. Please bear with me, friends.

After today's lesson, I intend for each lesson hereafter to give a presentation and explanation of the Bible. Yesterday's and today's lessons, however, are meant as an introduction to this. As stated above they show,

- the malady
- the physician
- the cure

Starting tomorrow we will begin offering the cure. But back to today's lesson.

The opening description of my blog site reads, *Jesus insisted, "You must be born again" [John 3:3]. Liberal Christians won't go there; evangelical Christians stop there: Jesus starts there!* That, friends, is my estimate of the situation. It portrays the problem.

I have no axe to grind when it comes to any Christian church or denomination. Truth be told, all of us Christians were condemned sinners, now saved by grace. We did nothing to earn our way to heaven, and we don't deserve it. I have my own maladies for God to heal. I don't think I am "preaching" from atop Mount Zion, with my head in the clouds and my "superiority" worn on my sleeves.

Rather, I am hanging my head in shame over my sins, and I mean to exhort other Christians to do the same over their own. But I haven't any individual(s) in mind when I do this. This is not meant to be a personal vendetta of any sort: it is a prophet sounding the alarm to those he is meant to love and serve.

What do I mean when I state, *Jesus insisted, "You must be born again"?...evangelical Christians stop there?* When a baby is born, his food is milk. So, too, does Scripture use this symbolism: *Like newborn babies, long for the pure milk of the word, so that by it you may grow in respect to salvation* [1 Peter 2:2]. The "newborn babies" terminology Peter used demonstrates he was writing to new Christians; so they needed to feed on milk, just as babies do in the natural realm.

Yet babies are not noted for remaining babies and drinking milk throughout the decades of their earthly existence! It's only a matter of months before they start cutting teeth and desiring nutrition of more substance than just straight liquids. They don't have to try to cut teeth, neither be exhorted to cut teeth, nor be taught to cut teeth: teeth cutting comes automatically by nature. In fact, I've never even heard of a case where a human has had some kind of deficiency which prevents him or her from having teeth. It might be a rare occurrence, but I've not heard of it.

So drinking only milk and never eating solid food for years and decades is utterly unnatural. It's a sign that something is rotten in the state of Denmark! On this point also Scripture is emphatic:

> *For though by this time you ought to be teachers, you need someone to teach you the elementary truths of God's word all over again. You have need again for someone to teach you the elementary principles of the oracles of God, and you have come to need milk and not solid food! For*

everyone who partakes only of milk is not accustomed to the word of righteousness, for he is an infant. But solid food is for the mature, who because of practice have their senses trained to discern good from evil [Hebrews 5:12-14; cf., 1 Corinthians 3:2].

Again we are told by God that milk is for babies, spiritually as well as naturally speaking. And we saw in 1 Peter 2:2 that baby Christians need "spiritual milk"—or as the New American Standard Bible translates it, "the pure milk of the word".

You see, the Christian's "spiritual food" is the Word of God. Spiritual food does not refer to teachings or doctrines about the Bible; nor does it point to little Sunday School ditties or daily devotional booklets about the Bible; neither does it embrace books that claim to tell us how to get right with God in four (or forty) easy lessons—even if the book is on the New York Times bestsellers list for umpteen cudzillion days!

Friends, the Christian's spiritual food is the b-i-b-l-e, BIBLE. Secondhand and thirdhand testimony about the Bible will not do. Some sort of Readers Digest consolidation of the Bible won't do. A Sunday sermon consisting of a verse here or there torn out of **context** will not do. Those methods will only serve to starve us into perpetual babyhood.

Each Christian needs to feed on the Bible daily, even as he feeds on natural food daily. And feeding on the Bible means just that, viz., the Bible—not this and that verse or this and that chapter or this and that book, but all of it from Genesis through Revelation!

As Paul told the Ephesian elders when he last saw them:

Therefore, I testify to you this day that I am innocent of the blood of all men. For I did not shrink from declaring to you the whole purpose of God. Be on guard for yourselves and for all the flock, among which the Holy Spirit has made you overseers, to shepherd the church of God which He purchased with His own blood. I know that after my departure savage wolves will come in among you, not sparing the flock; and from among your own selves men will arise, speaking perverse things, to draw away the disciples after them. Therefore be on the alert, remembering that night and day for a period of three years I did not cease to admonish each one with tears [Acts 20:26-31].

Paul gave these beloved children-become-leaders his last will and testament. And what was it that concerned him the most at this his final meeting with them on earth? Only this, that the leadership of the church might not give the flock the full-course meal God provided for them, but that they would pick and choose what to eat and what to feed the flock.

With liberal Christianity we get an avoidance of spiritual food (the Bible). With evangelical Christianity we get a malnutritious diet of a verse out of Timothy one Sunday, a verse or two out of Genesis the next Sunday, a few verses from Psalms the following Sunday, etc. etc. ad nauseam ad infinitum! And the **context** for the verses is not even considered, much less sufficiently explained; so our understanding of what the text teaches is automatically handicapped right off the bat.

Paul's comments, as just quoted, reveal the results of such a course of study: outside wolves and inside snakes in the grass will find a ready audience to subvert the work of God in the church. "So be on your guard!" Paul exhorted. Friends, we need the whole counsel of God. That is what this book and the entire *Heavenly Citizens* series will attempt to provide over the course of the following years.

Before concluding today, let us refer back one more time to the *Book of Hebrews*. I quoted above from chapter 5 that, if we've been Christians for any length of time at all, we shouldn't still be drinking spiritual milk: we should be feeding on solid spiritual meat and therefore able to teach others the Word (cf., Hebrews 5:12-14).

Chapter 6 of Hebrews goes on to tell us what this means:

> *Therefore leaving the elementary teaching about the Christ, let us press on to maturity, not laying again a foundation of repentance from dead works and of faith toward God, of instruction about washings and laying on of hands, and the resurrection of the dead and eternal judgment* (verses 1-2).

It is as if to say, "Stop sipping milk from Mommy's breast and start chewing meat!"

Milk is defined as "the elementary teachings about Christ". It is not that we are to deny these or stop remembering them. Rather, we are to stop being satisfied with this knowledge and to *grow in the grace and knowledge of our Lord and Savior Jesus Christ* [2 Peter 3:18]. We are to add more substance to our beginner's knowledge and stop the baby steps. The foundation was laid when we were **born again**: now we must build our lives on this foundation by feeding on the whole counsel of God and applying what we learn to our lives.

This raises some obvious questions like, "Just what is the whole counsel of God?" and, "How do I apply it to my life?" That, dear friends, is what the following articles are about, viz., an exposition of the Scriptures in **context**, with each book from first word to last. It is only on the Bible itself that we feed and nourish our spiritual life and so grow up in Christ, you see (cf., Ephesians 4:15).

Before parting, allow me to add this excerpt from my book:

This (book) is designed as food for the newborn Christian and for the Christian who has not yet gone to solid food. Consequentially, I will not as a rule make reference to the Hebrew or Greek words in the original manuscripts; nor will I attempt to be thorough and exhaust all avenues of knowledge for any given text.

I intend not to do research on any of the Scriptures before writing these (articles), lest I become entangled in the love for more and deeper feeding and thus give myself my pleasures, all the while losing the younger Christians who need discipled.

All texts will not be treated with equal length: the goal is for the young Christian, who may perhaps feel overwhelmed when opening his or her Bible, to be aided in beginning this journey into the whole counsel of God. Some texts will make these dear souls erudite, while other texts are esoteric at their stage of growth.

I exhort those who read these lessons to have their Bible opened to the text at hand, and to always compare what I explain with the text itself. Don't take my word or anyone else's word for it: the Bible is our sole and final authority in all matters of faith and practice. Let the journey begin, and God be with us.

C. How, And How Not, To Study The Bible

In our last lesson I stated my intention to begin our study with James 1:1 today; but subsequent thoughts occurred to me which need to be addressed. This is best done before beginning with our Bible analysis, rather than making frequent stops in order to interject tangential ideas piecemeal into the analysis. So let us begin the pursuit.

Consider what happens when we read any book other than the Bible. We first determine the book's style of writing, e.g., history book, novel, poetry, fiction or non-fiction, (for our particularly erudite folks) comic book (ha ha).

If we are reading poetry, we know there is a thing called "poetic license". When the Bible in a poetry section refers to "the circle of the earth" (Isaiah 40:22), for instance, we recognize that it is not trying to teach us that the earth is round: it is simply poetic expression. Or when we read in Scripture how God will hide us under His wings (Psalm 91:4), we know God is Spirit and spirits don't have physical wings. This is poetry, and it is not to be taken literally unless the **context** clearly supports its literalness.

However, when the context does support the literal interpretation, we must interpret it literally. Imagine someone says, "My neighbor next door is a dastardly fiend. He blasts his stereo into the wee hours of the morning, and I can't sleep! I'm gonna kill him!" Normally I would interpret it as frustration, a letting off of steam, but definitely not his plan to dispatch the neighbor to meet his Maker!

Yet if, on the other hand, he stated those same words with uncontrollable rage in his voice, and his demeanor reinforced that impression, and if he were waving around a .45 magnum in one hand and a machete in the other and describing how he would first empty the gun's bullets into the neighbor's brain and then cut off the skull—I believe under those conditions I would take it literally!

Do you see the difference? Of course you do! We face these sorts of distinctions daily. It is called "context". Which brings us to my number one rule for Bible interpretation (or any other interpretation, for that matter): *a text without a context is a pretext.* Memorize it. Apply it. Live by it. A text without a **context** is a pretext. Period.

Consider your kids in high school. Suppose one of them goes to English class and the teacher says, "We've been reading chapter seven of *Great Expectations*, and today it's time for us to analyze it. Johnny, what happened in chapter seven?"

In response Johnny offers, "Well, Ms. Charles, I think it means..." and he goes on for a while about what he thinks.

Teacher then asks Sandy, Ken, Barbie, and others to interpret the chapter, and each of them has an opinion.

Friends, I can't speak for you, but I would be up in arms if Ms. Charles' response to all this was to say, "Very good, teenagers. Each of your opinions is as good as anyone else's. Go your way and continue being opinionated." Yes, folks, that is just what such behaviors amount to, viz., being opinionated.

Great Expectations (and every other novel) is to be understood by what the author meant, and is to be interpreted according to the literal words (allowing for the poetic license we already noted). Words don't mean just anything you or I want them to mean: they have specific definitions and are to be understood accordingly.

The teenagers in my illustration would turn out to be contemporary ignoramuses, if they were "taught" that way in school—which, unfortunately, might well explain the inferior education ranking among the world's developed countries which America's young folks now hold. Ms. Charles needed to be educated enough herself to understand what *Great Expectations* does mean, and to pass on this information to her students. Is that not the essence of "teaching"?

So what does that have to do with this book? Just this: when it comes to Bible interpretation, I've often heard folks in the more liberally-inclined churches assert how their opinion is as good as mine. Truth be told, they are absolutely correct. When it comes to Bible interpretation, everyone's opinion is as good as the next person's—because all of our opinions are worthless!

God's "opinion" and His alone is what matters, and His "opinion" is given to us in the Bible. The words of the Bible have specific meaning, and the sentences have specific meaning, and the paragraphs and chapters have specific meaning, and the entire individual books have specific meaning.

Our job is not to have our opinion (which is simply to be opinionated). Our job is to learn how to understand the meaning of the words and phrases and sentences etc., and then apply this understanding to our lives. That is what the phrase "Jesus is Lord" means. His Word, His will, His glory, not mine. And so we've come full circle once again and returned to the Bible (and the reason for this book).

Another frequent type of anomalous reasoning I've heard from Christians—but this time from the evangelical wing—basically winds up in the same outfield as the prior reasoning, but with a more pious ring to it. It goes like this: "The Bible isn't the most important thing; the Holy Spirit is. **You** may know your Bible, but **I** hear the Holy Spirit talk to me."

Let me be clear, pointed, and unequivocal in my reply to this, friends: bah, humbug! Seriously, though, this is specious reasoning of the sorriest sort, a false dichotomy of a fiendish nature, pious balderdash which convinces only those who really don't know and understand the Bible. Let me sound the warning to all who will listen: whenever anyone talks about the Holy Spirit apart from the Bible, FLEE! There is no such thing, at least so far as the issue relates to us humans still here in time and space.

Yes, the Holy Spirit can and does talk to us apart from the Bible. If you know Jesus as Savior and are growing in Him (which is via the Bible), the Spirit will lead you throughout your life (as, for instance, when we prayerfully consider careers, ministry, etc.). The distinction here is that those are personal issues. And even for suchlike issues we must know our Bible, if we would not listen to false voices and personal preferences and think these things are the Holy Spirit leading us.

You might tell me, "The Holy Spirit has called me to the mission field." I can believe it or not, but that is inconsequential. If you believe it to be your calling, you need to walk by faith and act on it and tune out adversity and other folks' discouragement. Hopefully, under this belief though, you have shown the ability to do missions work and adjust to another culture, if you are going to another one.

But if you stand up in the church and say, "Thus says the Holy Spirit!"—friend, you had best have Scriptural warrant to show that the Spirit does indeed have such teachings and exhortings, or else you need to sit down and keep the peace. Which again brings us full-circle to…our Bibles.

The Holy Spirit does not shout from heaven, "Randy, thus says the Lord!" Everything God wants us to know for all matters of faith and practice has already been "spoken" to us via the Bible. He already recorded everything He wants us to know. Since He is a God of order and not confusion (1 Corinthians 14:33), and since He is not man that He should change His mind (Numbers 23:19), He doesn't have to add to it or take away from it. *The Bible is our sole and final authority in all matters of faith and practice*, until such time as Jesus comes again and we see Him face to face.

Of course, as per 1 Corinthians 2, we need the mind of the Spirit to understand the things of God. Just intellectually studying the Bible doesn't assure us of understanding it as God wants us to. This is why I earlier identified this objection as a false dichotomy. We do need the Holy Spirit to understand the Bible. The Bible is God's Word to man, His thoughts and desires for us. He needs to explain Himself, rather than we assume with our natural minds that we can understand Him and don't need His Spirit but only His Book.

Notwithstanding all that, again, the Holy Spirit does not shout from heaven or sneak up behind us and suggest in our ears what He wants us to know. Such an understanding is not to be found (or even intimated) anywhere in the entire Bible! The Bible teaches (e.g., John 14-16) how the Holy Spirit was sent by Jesus to His saints to lead them into all truth and to remind them of the things He said. Now that we have all those thoughts and words of His written down as the Bible, the Holy Spirit takes it and explains it to us.

Again we come full-circle back to the Bible (and the reason for this book). Therefore it is a false dichotomy to demand either (1) the Holy Spirit or else (2) the Bible. God's chosen way for us is to be saved by means of His Word as the Holy Spirit applies it to our hearts and we respond affirmatively to it from the heart. *For by grace are you saved through faith* [Ephesians 2:8]. *Faith comes from hearing, and hearing by the word of Christ* [Romans 10:17]. We must have the Word of God to have faith.

The very definition of *faith* is that God said it, and we believe it and act accordingly. Unless we hear what He says (i.e., the Bible), we cannot have faith. If we hear the Bible but it only enters our heads (intellectual affirmation) and not our hearts (spiritual transformation via the Holy Spirit), then we haven't Biblical faith and the Word is not living in us.

Thus we need the Bible in our heads, and we need the Holy Spirit to move us to conviction and repentance and a new heart. But it all begins with hearing the Bible, so that the Holy Spirit has God's chosen resource in us (viz., His Word) as the raw material for enlivening us.

What we humans (including us Christians) want is to have our own way. That is the definition of sin. God gives us His rules and, like babies straight from the womb, the first words we learn are "No! I won't!" The answer to that mentality is "Jesus is Lord, not me!" "Have Your way, Master." *He must increase, but I must decrease* [John 3:30].

Am I rambling now? What does this have to do with my book? Well, I've seen from us Christians over and over again that we don't let God interpret our lives and our living. Rather, we interpret God (i.e., His Word) according to our lives. In the church this appears in various behaviors and attitudes.

For example, if the church is in need of a pastor, we pass around a questionnaire asking the congregation what specifics they want in the next pastor. Voilà! classic humanism: life revolves around man, not God.

The spiritual procedure would be for us to delve into the Bible (how'd that get in here again?) and examine the qualifications for a pastor. By following this procedure we learn what God wants, not what man wants. And we are to interpret the Bible's qualifications according to the literal meaning of the words, and within the **context** of the times and cultures in which they were written. From there we draw out the principals involved and then make an application of the principles to our contemporary culture.

Another common example of humanism in the church is when we revolve the concepts of "good" and "bad" around our own feelings and wants. Like when someone is nice to me; therefore that person is a great Christian, filled with the Spirit no doubt. But, beware! If he should look askance at me or not give me the amount of attention I think I deserve, what a vagabond and wolf-in-sheep's-clothing he becomes!

When it comes to determining the definition of "spiritual", such an approach produces catastrophic consequences. Folks are termed "spiritual" when they smile all the time (they must have the "joy of the Lord" if they do so), and are "positive" all the time (God wants to lift our spirits, not put us down), and generally seem pleasant and make everybody in the church happy. Amen, brethren. That sounds like true spirituality to me! (Pardon the sarcasm, please.)

Actually, if you open your Bible (it has crept into this book once again!) and turn to 1 Kings 22 (as one example of many), you will see how that kind of behavior was very common in Biblical times. Trouble is, the behavior wasn't what God's man-of-the-day exemplified: it was the behavior of the false prophets! In the Scriptures God is "negative" far more often than He is "positive". This is because He deals with sinful man in rebellion against Him.

"But wait!" I hear someone exclaim. "We're the church, the Christians. We're not sinful man. So we should always be positive."

Read your New Testament epistles, please, my friend, and observe how often Paul had to be "negative" to the Christians in the church. Christians are still sinners, though saved by grace. We have a new nature (the divine nature, just as Jesus has), but we still have the human nature (just as Jesus has)—the difference being that Jesus' human nature is sinless, while we Christians have the same human nature we had before being **born again**.

We will continue to have it until Jesus comes again in the **Rapture** (cf., 1 Thessalonians 4:13-18; 1 Corinthians 15:51-58). At that time we will receive our new resurrection body—we already have our new resurrection spirit—and thereafter through all eternity we will no longer have a traitor inside us driving us with a whip and saying, "Commit sin! Follow me and sin!"

"Spirituality" must not be based on what seems right or pleasing or sensible to me—that is the definition of walking by sight, and it is the way of the world and the flesh, humanism—but on the Bible (oops! it crept into this book again). Pastors are first and foremost required by God to lead the saints through the whole counsel of God, so they can discover the spiritual gifts given them by the Holy Spirit (1 Corinthians 12:7-11; Ephesians 4:11-17), and then use these gifts in the church. That is how the body of Christ is built up together to function in its fullness and accomplish all of God's purposes, and not man's.

If the Holy Spirit gives the gift, how dare anyone refuse its usage in the church! The church belongs to Jesus as Lord, not to the pastor or the deacons or the barn boss in the back pew. And *the gifts and the calling of God are irrevocable* [Romans 11:29].

But alas, we Christians want our own way. So we fill the pews with folks who don't "offend" us, and who make us feel good, and who therefore must be "spiritual". If we would have revival in our lives and in the church, dear people, we individually, and we as leaders and motivators in the church, must get back to the Bible, the whole Bible, and nothing but the Bible. The Bible is the authority for defining "spirituality". We must learn it and live it.

There is always so much more to be said, but let me leave off saying it at this point. We will take up the *Book of James* in our next study, God willing. In the meantime let us strive to grow in the grace and knowledge of our Lord and Savior Jesus Christ.

The Book of James: An Introduction – Part 1

Today we begin our exposition of the *Book of James*. In the last volume of our *Heavenly Citizens* series, we completed our studies of the Apostle Paul's contribution to the New Testament canon. The remaining epistles are before us. Let us not grow weary and lose heart. The light of God's Word beckons us onward and upward. Let us be faithful in taking up the pursuit, and walk in the light while it is still day.

The first task at hand is to identify the writer of this splendid letter. It makes the most sense to begin with the apostles, and here's why. The one ministry which the apostles had, and no one else did, was to serve as the official ambassadors of King Jesus.

An ambassador receives from the king (or the president) what his boss wants said; then the ambassador goes to the person to whom the king wants the message delivered and speaks the words of the king. The words and ideas of the ambassador do not enter the equation, not even in the slightest. No one cares. The king (or the president) is in charge. All other folks serve at his pleasure.

What does this have to do with the *Book of James*? We heard you wondering that loudly and clearly, so don't try denying it. It's like this. The Bible is the Word of God, the Word of King Jesus. Jesus personally chose twelve men from His disciples and appointed them to the office of **apostle**. As His apostles (aka ambassadors), they received the Word of the King (aka the Word of God) and passed it on to God's people as His authority to us, His people.

In other words all of the words of the New Testament were given by God (i.e., inspired by the Holy Spirit). God delivered these words through His apostles (aka His ambassadors), who committed them to writing for posterity's sake. Either an apostle wrote a New Testament document, or his disciple passed on his words for him.

Any other ministry function of an apostle was shared by other offices in the Church. Prophets prophesied along with apostles. Evangelists evangelized along with apostles. Pastors pastored along with apostles. The other Church offices requiring *speaking gifts* shared in parts of the job description of an apostle.

But nary a one of them received the official Word of God for His people directly from God, for the purpose of it being committed to writing as a part of the New Testament canon. Only the King's official ambassadors, the apostles, were personally chosen by the King for this ministry function.

This is why, when we go to determine the author of this official document in the New Testament, we begin with the apostles. Well lo and behold, there are two apostles who wore the name "James". Which one of them wrote this letter? Perhaps we had best add right quickly, or was it someone else who wrote it? If it was someone other than the two apostles named "James", then from which apostle did this other person receive the Word of the King and commit it to writing as the *Book of James*?

The two apostles named "James" were,

1.   James the son of Zebedee (Matthew 10:2)
2.   James the son of Alphaeus (Matthew 10:3)

The first "James" was the brother of the Apostle John. Jesus gave these two dudes the nickname "Boanerges", which means "sons of thunder" (cf., Mark 3:17). No reason is given in Mark 3 for why Jesus gave them the nickname. We suggest that, at the time the name was given, it was prophetic.

This is borne out further on in these two brother apostles' lives. The apostles were following Jesus on His ministry trek. When they passed through Samaria, the Samaritans refused to receive Jesus into their village because He was heading to Jerusalem. Apostles James and John waxed eloquent, mimicking Prophet Elijah thusly:

Lord, do You want us to command fire to come down from heaven and consume them? [Luke 9:54]

How's that for a behavior from folks named "sons of thunder"? Today we would be inclined to name them "thunder mouths"!

Though it is possible that either of the two apostles named "James" could have written this letter, neither of them fit the bill very well. James the son of Zebedee was killed by King Herod circa 43 A.D. (cf., Acts 12:1-2). Though we have no exact date in Scripture for when the *Book of James* was written, most of the evidence used in dating it points to circa 49 A.D. or later. James ben Zebedee had been dead for over five years by that time, so he was in no condition to do any writing!

The reason for rejecting James ben of Alphaeus as the author is twofold. First, we know nothing about him. Scripture is silent vis-a-vis his person, so we haven't much to go on vis-à-vis his writing skills. Secondly, we have a much more viable, indeed almost certain, candidate for the authorship of this Bible book. Yes, neither of those reasons outright excludes James ben of Alphaeus as the author; but who wants to bet on second or third best option, when a first best is available? Not us, and we hope not you either!

Before introducing you to the obvious choice of author for the *Book of James*, let us date this letter. Our reasoning for doing so at this time is that the date of the letter helps eliminate some of the candidates for authorship. We already saw that James ben Zebedee was dead at the likely time of this letter's writing, for example.

Three paragraphs prior we stated that circa 49 A.D. was the most accepted date. What we failed to do back then was give any reasons for such a conclusion. Let's make it our task at this juncture of our exposition.

Bible scholars provide great quantities of evidence which they use in dating the *Book of James*. For our purposes here, we will limit the information to a concise blip of two details from Scripture, rather than a multitude of paragraphs. These two are,

1. the Judaizer heresy (*Book of Galatians*)
2. the Jerusalem Council (Acts 15)

The Judaizer heresy refers to Jewish Pharisees who thought to accept Jesus as the Messiah. Ergo, they saw themselves as believers in the Church. Trouble was, they didn't believe in the "Jesus" of Scripture.

The Jews, and all the world, back in the day thought of the Messiah as a Jewish military conqueror. He would suddenly appear and lead the Jews to military victory over the Romans and all the rest of the Gentiles. The word "Gentiles" means "nations" or "peoples". There was God's one and only "nation", Israel, you see. All the rest of the world consisted of the devil's "nations" (aka the Gentiles). Hence the constant contrast throughout *Tanakh* (aka the Old Testament) between the Jews and the Gentiles.

So the Jews' concept of the Messiah was that of a Jewish military figure, who would lead the Jews to world domination over the Gentiles. Ergo, when some of the Pharisees accepted Jesus as the Jewish Messiah, they still thought in terms of the "nation" of Israel and world domination.

Under that scenario, the "nation" of Israel, with its land and Law (aka *Torah*, or the Law of Moses), still reigned supreme in God's plan of salvation. The "saving" consisted of foisting on the entire world the Covenant of Law as God's Word. The Jews would be saved from their conquered state under Roman rule; the Gentiles would be saved by becoming Jewish proselytes, with the Jews ruling over them.

A Jewish proselyte was a Gentile who observed the Word of God, as it was put in practice by the Jews. He saw that it was moral, while all of the Gentile religions were immoral. This Gentile noted the one God of Israel with His justice vs. the innumerable gods of the Gentiles with their flagitious madness and injustice.

So he renounced his Gentile heritage and adopted Judaism as his new life. This began with being circumcised, and then committing to follow the entirety of *Torah* (aka the Law of Moses). To do so, this erstwhile Gentile, but now Jewish proselyte, moved to Israel to live as a Jew. In Jesus' day Gentiles in Gentile lands—who converted to Judaism through the Jewish community and synagogue of their home town—lived as a Jew in the Jewish community, following all of the Jewish customs in vogue at the time.

In fine, the Judaizers thought to accept Jesus as the Messiah, and crown Him atop the Covenant of Law like a cherry on top of a sundae! In Scripture Messiah Jesus fulfilled the Law in toto, so Jews are no longer obligated to attempt obedience to it. In the case of Gentiles, any and all of their ideas about being good enough to please God (i.e., morality and religion) are now null and void too.

Jews and Gentiles alike, who receive Jesus as their Messiah and Savior, no longer are to attempt to be good enough to please God. Jesus did this for us! We already live with God as being pleasing to Him "in Christ". Because we who are saved are "in Christ", we live the new life of Christ in us, the hope of glory (cf., Colossians 1:27). The life we now live in the flesh, we live by faith in the son of God (cf., Galatians 2:20).

Instead of walking by sight and doing what seems right in our own eyes (i.e., eating fruit from the **kogae tree)**, we walk by faith and do what is right in Jesus' eyes (i.e., eat fruit from the **life tree**). This the Judaizers refused to do. Their concept was to walk over to the life tree (aka Jesus the Word of God) and sample a bite of the fruit. Then they spent the rest of the day under the shade of the kogae tree, where they savored the flavor of man's words about God's Word (the Pharisees' manmade doctrines).

There is no mention, or even insinuation, of the Judaizer heresy in the *Book of James*. The Apostle Paul attacks it mercilessly in the *Book of Galatians*, which was written circa 55-57 A.D. However, the Judaizer invasion of the Galatian churches occurred years before that date, viz., circa 51 A.D. and later (the time of Paul's second missions trip). Ergo, the *Book of James* would appear to have been written prior to 51 A.D.

Even more, the Jerusalem Council (cf., Acts 15) occurred circa 50 A.D. Paul planted the churches of Galatia on his first missions trip, circa 45-47 A.D. The Judaizers wasted no time after Paul moved on from Galatia, in invading the Galatian churches and peddling their heretical wares. This led to the Jerusalem Council, where both sides (Paul and the Judaizers) were heard. The decision of this Church Council was that the Judaizers were heretics and the true Gospel was presented by the Apostle Paul.

The date of the Jerusalem Council is one year sooner than the beginning of Paul's second missions trip, viz., circa 50 A.D. Yet even with this earlier date, the Apostle James ben Zebedee was already dead for seven years. So he is eliminated from the list of potential authors of the *Book of James*.

Even more, with no mention, or even an intimation, of the Judaizer heresy or the Jerusalem Council in the *Book of James*, the most likely reason is that this Bible book was written prior to those two details. And what details they are too! The fate of the Gospel hung in the balance! How could any Spirit-filled apostle or disciple ignore such matters, when writing a doctrinal letter to the Jewish believers of those days? Conclusion: the *Book of James* preceded the Judaizer heresy and the Jerusalem Council, which suggests a likely dating around 49 A.D. or sooner.

With those amenities out of the way, we may now return to the issue of which "James" penned the letter. The most likely culprit, er, we mean author, was James, a half-brother of the Lord Jesus (cf., Matthew 13:55). Prior to Jesus' crucifixion and burial, His brothers were unbelievers (cf., John 7:5). After Jesus rose out of death, however, His brothers became believers (cf., Acts 1:14).

Jesus' "brothers" were actually "half-brothers" because Jesus' had no human father, while his "brothers" did. Jesus was miraculously conceived by the Holy Spirit in the Jewish virgin, Miriam (cf., Matthew 1:20). This makes Jesus to have <u>both</u> the nature of God <u>and</u> the nature of man in on Person. Jesus is the God-Man.

This is why Jesus, and only Jesus, is able to save to the uttermost any sinful person who comes to Him for God's salvation, the only true salvation (cf., Hebrews 7:25). This is why Jesus is the only way to the Father (cf., John 14:6). This is why there is no other name under heaven whereby we must be saved (cf., Acts 4:12).

Jesus' half-brother not only became a believer within the first fifty days after Jesus rose out of death (cf., Acts 1:14), but he remained steadfast in his faith "in Christ". We know this because the Bible tells us so. Yes, we know it's a children's song. But it's the truth, so what the hey. We're speaking spiritual truth.

Where in the Bible does it tell us that Jesus' half-brother James remained steadfast in his faith "in Christ", you are wondering about now? Ai yai yai! There y'all go with the wondering again! Read Acts 15 and see for yourselves. Jesus' half-brother James was Pastor James in the First Church of Jerusalem (cf., Galatians 1:19). How's that for remaining steadfast in his faith "in Christ"?

Judging by Scripture—in Logic 101 it is known as an *argumentum ex silentio*, or an *argument from silence* for short—but Scripture only reveals this James as being in Jerusalem. Based on this we suggest that the *Book of James* was written by him from Jerusalem.

Oh, but we're not done just yet! The Jerusalem Council of Acts 15 served to expose the Judaizer heresy as weeds and not true wheat, as man's words and not God's Word. Pastor James, the Lord's half-brother, sent this letter to the churches in Gentile lands which the Apostle Paul planted. The letter is based on the conclusions of the official Church Council in Jerusalem (cf., Acts 15:23-29).

A comparison of this letter with the *Book of James* intimates that Pastor James is both the author of the Jerusalem Council letter and the *Book of James*. Consider these examples in your Bible:

- (Acts 15:23 vs. James 1:1) both letters begin, "Greetings!"
- (Acts 15:13 vs. James 2:5) nearly identical in both letters
- (Acts 15:29 vs. James 1:27) quite similar Jewish concepts
- the Jerusalem Council letter was written to Jewish and Gentile believers in Gentile lands; the *Book of James* was written to the Jewish believers in churches in Gentile lands (cf., James 1:1[b])

Those tidbits should serve to whet your appetite for more spiritual truth. Carefully peruse both letters and find the many comparisons to be made. We will speak more fully on the comparison in the last bullet, when we study verse 1[b]. But for now let's practice patience, even while we are champing at the bit. Oh, and about Bullet #1:in Scripture only James begins a letter with "Greetings!" Let's pray.

The Book of James: An Introduction – Part 2

In Part 1 of this *Introduction* we addressed the issues of who wrote the *Book of James*, when it was written, and to whom it was written.

Another question to ask prior to explicating the actual text of the letter is, "Why was this letter written?" Some folks have proffered the novel concept that the letter was written to ward off the false teachings known as *antinomianism*. Stop that! Take off your befuddled face this instant! We'll define terms for you. No need to fret your pretty face over it.

The term *antinomianism* comes from the Greek: *anti* (against) + *nomos* (law) = "against law". But what does it all mean? Really? You are wondering again? Slow down and let me catch up, y'all!

It's like this. Some professed believers back in the day (and today too!) thought that, since Jesus saves us from the Law and we are free "in Christ", believers don't have to follow any more laws. And they omit nothing from the list either! Let's enumerate and see:

1. *Torah* (aka the Law of Moses)? we're free from it
2. the U.S. Constitution & legal code? nope, we're free
3. legalism in the Church? we're still free
4. morality? free free free!

But, you know, it is highly unlikely that James, a believing Jew of Bible times, would write to other believing Jews for the purpose of exhorting them not to be anarchists! That's what being totally "free" from any and all law amounts to. It's every person for himself, so watch out!

Biblical Jews were steeped in legalism. Law and morality was their daily bread. All of this being the case, warning such folks about *antinomianism* seems a bit of a stretch—a humongous "bit" at that! No thank you. We think we'll pass on that interpretation of the *Book of James*.

During the 1st Century A.D., the Church faced incredible amounts of persecution. It was standard fare for believers in both the Promised Land and in the Gentile lands. The *Book of Hebrews* was written because of this issue. The Jewish believers in the city of Jerusalem, and in all of the Promised Land, were tempted to hide their faith in Jesus and return to the temple and synagogue. Then the Jewish authorities and their sycophants might leave them alone.

The writer to the Hebrews exhorted them to be faithful to Christ. Believers are *heavenly citizens in earthly shoes*. Believers are to keep their eyes on Jesus, the Author and Perfecter of faith. Any persecution which believers face pales in comparison with what Messiah Jesus endured on our behalf. So don't look at the persecutors and surrender. Persevere in the faith, O believers!

The author of the *Book of James* wrote in the same vein. As we study this Bible book, we will see how he exhorts Jewish believers in Gentile lands to be steadfast in living out their faith in Jesus which God has already worked in them (cf., Philippians 2:12-13). You may wish to study *Philippians* and *Hebrews* with us. Copies available at https://randyg555.wixsite.com/heavenly-citizens/shop.

Yep, the more likely purpose for James writing this letter is as plain as the nose on our face. As pastor of the Jerusalem Church, which was Jewish in toto, James exhibited the Jewish (Oriental) approach to thinking and logic, as it relates to God and spiritual matters.

For Orientals, the fruit of our life is presented as being illustrative of the true root and vine which make up a person. We can see our works and hear our words, but we cannot see our heart. No one can even see his own heart, much less anyone else's. So the Oriental chooses to stick with what he can see right in front of him.

The Greek/Gentile (Occidental) approach is speculative. We are inquisitive about why and how people and things are who or what they are. This goes to the root and vine (the heart) which grows the fruit of our life (the words and works which we can hear and see). The Occidental speculates, "Just because I spoke a few evil words doesn't mean I'm evil. I'm really a fine fellow at heart, you know." Jesus the Oriental (James too!) refutes such claptrap. We will see James do it as we progress through this Bible book. Listen now to Jesus do it:

> *A good tree cannot produce bad fruit, nor can a bad tree produce good fruit* [Matthew 7:18; read verses 15-23].

See! We Occidentals have a standing invitation for ol' Aristotle to come for supper. He sits with us at the dinner table and croons us with his riveting logic. Such frequent visitations from him, and small wonder we are captured hook, line, and sinker.

> *Why looky at me, ma! Ain't I the dandy one? I may enjoy every vice on Planet Earth, but underneath it all I have a good heart. Truly I do, ma. You know I do.*

Being the loving mother she is, good ol' ma vocally asseverates her concurrence with such logic. Then she promptly reminds Mr. Aristotle to hurry back again. After all, who can challenge his fascinating logic? No one, of course. After all, no one can see the heart, so who can denounce it as evil?

Uh, Jesus can. Just reread Matthew 7:15-23 once more and see. He can...and He does! And at the Great White Throne judgment, everyone who didn't come to Jesus and confess his evil heart to Him, Jesus will judge to be eternally evil. Consequently, such folks will spend eternity separated from God, forever enjoying the company of his/her evil heart.

All of this being spiritual truth—as it surely is—James speaks to the believer's newfound faith in Jesus, his eternal life, identifying it as a practical matter—as contrasted with an abstract theory about what cannot be seen. That is the Oriental approach (Pastor James) vs. the Occidental approach (Philosopher Aristotle). James puts shoe leather to the classroom teaching about "faith". James doesn't deny "faith" and substitute good works in its place. The two (faith resulting in works) go hand-in-hand, like a married couple: there is no true marriage without <u>both</u> husband <u>and</u> wife united as one.

Yes, spouses had best not be opposed to each other! Mr. Faith and Mrs. Works become one in holy matrimony. The Apostle Paul teaches this very thing in his New Testament letters. The first half of his letters generally contain doctrine, the second half practical application of the doctrine. In Scripture the concept of "doctrine" refers to the spiritual truth of eternity, as God teaches it to us in His Word. The believer's works are spiritual <u>only</u> when they are done in obedience to God's Word, as the Holy Spirit teaches it to us. We often express this in our *Heavenly Citizens* series like so:

> *Nothing spiritual ever transpires apart from [1]the Word of God and [2]the Holy Spirit.*

First we need to know who we are (doctrine), and then we can understand what we are to do (good works) and why we are to do them.

Messiah Jesus teaches this same concept as well. We saw an example of it a wee bit earlier (Matthew 7:15-23). We also see it from Jesus approach to rearing believers into disciples. He took His disciples along with Him as He ministered to people. The disciples heard His teaching (doctrine) and also witnessed His doing (works). The teaching = classroom instruction, the doing = on-the-job training. They learned who they were then lived it out.

In churches today some believers want to hear "plain-speak", so-called. They cannot stomach Bible truth, you see. Just point them to what needs to be done, and they'll do it, yes, they will. That is a classic example of the Oriental manner of thinking and logic, which the Israelites exhibited at Mt. Sinai.

Yahveh (aka the Lord) held His hand out with grace (the Ten Commandments), but they wouldn't take it! They complained to Moses that they didn't appreciate God's tone of voice. Strain your ears and grit your teeth, and you can hear them as they tell it:

> *If only God would talk in a way more to our liking, then we would listen to Him. So you, Moses, you go and listen to God's blaring, frightening voice; then come back and tell us what He wants us to do. We will do everything God tells us, all of it without fail! You tell God for us that we are good old boys and girls. We are quite capable of pleasing Him in our own power without any handouts.*

God's response was to give these urchins what they demanded of Him. Ladies and gentlemen, allow us to introduce to you *Torah* (aka the Law of Moses). It is the opposite of God's grace. The Law says, "First do, and then you will live!" God's grace counters, "First live, and then you will do!"

Biblical doctrine teaches us who we are as believers. We need to first be born again as <u>spiritual</u> new creations "in Christ". This equips us to do works which are actually <u>spiritual</u>. All of the teaching about being "spiritual" cannot be <u>shown</u> to be spiritual, should we not grow God's "good works" in our life. On the other hand, all of the "good works" in the world cannot make anyone the least bit "spiritual". First comes rebirth (spiritual life), and only then can—and must—"spiritual" good works follow from a true born again occurrence.

Law, both God's and man's, demands of folks what they are to do or not do; but law provides nothing to equip anyone to obey. God's grace already did everything we need done, and He offers it to us freely. Once we receive God's grace and become reborn children of God, then God's grace in us rears us to spiritual maturity. As spiritually mature disciples of King Jesus, our new nature performs good works, spiritual works. Spiritual works are always good. No other sort of works are ever good. And once again we remind you,

> *Nothing spiritual ever transpires apart from [1]the Word of God and [2]the Holy Spirit.*

Many a good believer has failed to make this distinction and fallen short of Pastor James' teaching in this Bible book. They fancy seeing James on stage with Paul—a sort of "presidential debate", if you would. Paul shouts at James in vehement dislike, "Study your Bible, James, you rogue!" James bellows back, "Faith without works is dead, you ding-a-ling!"

Such a thing never happened, brothers and sisters. We promise! Nor could it because James and Paul were spiritual buddies. They didn't disagree about the makeup of the Gospel. Paul went to the Gentile lands; so he explained the Gospel in a manner conducive to Gentile understanding and acceptance. James remained in the land of the Jews; so he explained the Gospel in a manner which was conducive to Jewish understanding and acceptance.

The Gospel = both Biblical faith + Biblical works. The first Biblical work required of any sinner is this:

> *Therefore they said to Him, "What shall we do, so that we may <u>work</u> the works of God?" Jesus answered and said to*

them, "This is the <u>work</u> of God, that you <u>believe</u> <u>in</u> <u>Him</u> whom He has sent." [John 6:28-29]

First a sinner—that's all of us—must be born again (spiritual rebirth). Only then can we proceed to live as born again. Didn't Jesus speak clearly enough to this matter, brothers and sisters? Why, then, all of the confusion in the assembly of believers?

Martin Luther didn't like James, no, not in the least bit. He labeled the *Book of James* "the epistle of straw"! He wanted to exclude it from the New Testament canon. Seriously.

Believe us when we say that Luther was a powerful man of God, not a heretic! Still, he was merely a man, not Jesus the God-Man. As all men have done and still do, they fall short of the glory of God. It happens, and it won't cease until our *glorification*. We'll have opportunities to expound on the concept of the believer's *glorification* later. For now let's leave it at that.

In this Bible book Pastor James mimics Jesus in His *Sermon on the Mount* approach (Matthew 5-7). Both the *Sermon on the Mount* and the *Book of James* are thoroughly Jewish. What else should we expect, since both Jesus and James were thoroughly Jewish? James wrote this Bible book as a Jew writing to other Jews.

Someone wonders about now, "Then why would we Gentiles bother learning the teachings found in the *Book of James*?

Consider it like this. Jews need to put into practice (i.e., <u>do</u>) these spiritual truths. Gentiles need to see past <u>knowing</u> spiritual truths, and move on to <u>doing</u> the spiritual truths they think they know. Because we Gentiles know the facts, we think we are spiritual.

Not so! Jesus taught us better. Study His *Parable of the Soils* and learn the lesson. The rocky soil (emotional faith) produced no good fruit. The thorn-infested soil (intellectual faith) produced no good fruit. (The beaten path didn't even "receive" God's Word.) Only the good soil produced any spiritual fruit at all!

All three soils received the seed of God's Word. But merely "receiving" God's Word ≠ being born again, and without rebirth nothing spiritual can occur. Biblical "receiving" (aka faith) occurs not when the seed of the Word grows only in the emotions and/or in the head. The seed of the Word must move into the heart and grow there, in order to be Biblical faith, saving faith, eternal life.

This is convicting spiritual truth we must hear and heed, brothers and sisters. So why do we stand here staring at one another? Let's dive into the *Book of James* and learn it! Come on.

James 1:1 (Part 1)

Immediately as we embark upon our trek through the *Book of James*, we are confronted with an issue which demands our attention. This is true of all the letters which comprise the New Testament canon. Let us explain.

Today our letters take the format,

- Salutation (e.g., Dear John)
- Body of the letter
- Closing (e.g., Yours truly, Me)

Not so with the New Testament letters, however. They didn't do things our way back in the day. They were noted for marching to the tune of another drummer. The paradigm for their letters began with the Closing, followed by the Salutation, with the Body of the letter being the caboose.

Let's apply this to the *Book of James*, shall we?

- Closing (verse 1[a])
- Salutation/Opening (verse 1[b])
- Body of the letter (James 1:2-5:20)

With these amenities out of the way, we can now dive into the deep end of the pool. There we will discover all of the amazing spiritual truth which the Holy Spirit wants to share with us. So why do you stand there staring at one another? Get on down to Egypt and buy us some grain! Ya' hear?

James, a bond-servant of God and of the Lord Jesus Christ (verse 1[a]).

And thar she blows, me mateys! The Closing in all its pristine beauty for your eyes to behold. Isn't she a dandy?

Stop that! We don't want to see your befuddled face. Waddaya mean you don't understand why the Closing of this letter comes at the beginning? Whew, boy. We just got done explaining it to you. Methinks y'all need to focus a bit better. (lol)

One more time, it's like this. Back in the day letters began with the Closing. Actually they began with their version of a Salutation, which we today know as the Closing. The problem, you see, isn't that we are right and they are wrong. The problem is that they did things differently than us…and they came first! So let's get rid of the befuddled faces and get with the program here. Okay?

In *The Book of James: An Introduction*, we addressed the issue of who the author, the person named "James", is. We concluded that the evidence available points to him being the half-brother of Messiah Jesus. If you require more substance than that at this juncture of the text, we direct you back to the *Introduction* for a refresher course.

The Greek noun for our English translation "James" is *Iakobos*. Drop the Greek "os" suffix, and we are left with *Iakob*. The Greek iota ("I") becomes an English "J", and the Greek kappa ("k") transforms into an English "c". Voilà! our English name "Jacob".

The Hebrew name for "James" is *Ya'akob*, from the Hebrew noun *aqeb* which means "a heel". During birth Jacob grabbed the "heel" of his older twin brother Esau. Hence the name "Jacob", which means supplanter or he who grabs the heel and trips up. Just a bit extra. But not to worry. There's no extra charge.

James identifies himself as a "bond-servant". The Greek word is *doulos*, which can also be translated as "servant" or "slave". Before proceeding further in the text, we would do well to get a handle on this issue. What exactly is the difference between a "slave", a "servant", and a "bond-servant"? Let's investigate.

A "slave" is a piece of property owned by his master. The master may be a merry old soul, like Old King Cole, and treat his slave respectfully; or he may be a tyrant who abuses the slave in any way he so desires. This is because a slave is a piece of property, with little-to-no legal regulations governing the master's treatment of the slave.

A "servant" is a hired hand who works for his "employer". The servant might receive room and board, perhaps even a bit of an allowance, depending on what he agrees to with his employer. A servant is not a piece of property. He isn't required to work for the employer for life. His wife and kids are not the property of the employer either.

A "bond-servant" is in a middle position between a "slave" and a "servant". He is not the master/employer's property, as is a slave. Still, he isn't free to depart the master/employer's service at any time he might choose to do so. He owes the master/employer a debt, and he agrees to work it off for an agreed amount of time in the master/employer's service. Practically speaking, he is sort of owned, but only for a given amount of time.

Torah (aka the Law of Moses) allowed for an Israelite to become a "bond-servant" to another Israelite. But a stipulation in *Torah* specified that, every seven years, such a one was to be released from his debt. In other words, the Israelite debtor had to work for his Israelite creditor to pay off the debt. He could not just up and leave before the debt was paid. But the Israelite creditor could not force this Israelite debtor to work for him longer than the seven-year time limit either.

Ergo, the Israelite debtor was neither a slave nor a servant. He was a bond-servant, required to work off his debt in the service of his Israelite creditor. After doing so for the maximum of seven-years, he was a free man, who would likely need to hire himself to another well-to-do Israelite as his servant to earn a living wage.

In the New Testament this Greek word (i.e., *doulos*) is at times translated by any of those three nouns we noted above. We prefer to recognize any believer's position with Christ as that of a bond-servant, not a servant or a slave. Our reasoning is to be found in what we explicated above.

We believers are not free to serve Jesus if we feel like it, and then hire ourselves out to someone else (aka a mere "servant"). Nor are we forced to remain with Jesus because He owns us as His property for all eternity. Every believer is indebted to Jesus for his very life, yes; but Jesus never forces anyone to be saved, nor does He force any believer to serve Him. Any service to Jesus must be given to Him willingly, and it must be given out of love to Jesus for who He is and what He has done and is doing for the believer. That is a bond-servant. We work to pay a <u>debt</u> <u>of</u> <u>love</u>.

Yes, all of us believers are "owned" by Jesus, and yes, all of us are indebted to Him with a debt we can never repay. All three nouns have their limitations. We are not trying to skirt the issue of the believer's relationship with Jesus by avoiding the nouns "slave" and "servant". We are not too proud to proclaim Jesus' ownership over us as His "slave", or to admit our responsibility to willingly serve Him as His "servant".

But we maintain that *Torah's* (aka the Law of Moses') stipulation (i.e., the *Year of Release* for Israelite bond-servants every seven years) is a **type** of the believer's relationship with King Jesus. The believer's relationship with Jesus is the **antitype** of that stipulation. We must individually agree to serve Jesus willingly. This service lasts for all of time, which is what the number "7" denotes in Scripture—as in the "7" days of creation occurring, and then a new week of "7" days begins again. All of time is composed of a 7-day period (aka a week), and then a new week of 7 days begins…and repeats all over again for 7 more days.

No, we don't serve Jesus for all of time, and then are released from serving Him in eternity. In eternity we are released from serving Jesus in the ministry we have here on earth. Through all of eternity we will serve Jesus in the ministry He assigns us at the *Bema* (aka the Judgment Seat of Christ for believers). Our ministry in eternity will be dependent on what reward(s) we receive from Him at the *Bema*, even as our ministry on earth for all of time is dependent on what ministry Jesus assigns us here, and the spiritual gifts the Holy Spirit furnishes us for performing this ministry.

Scriptural warrant about God's people being His bond-servants is to be had in many locations. Examples are,

- Philippians 2:7 (Jesus is God's bond-servant)
- James 1:1 (James is God's bond-servant)
- Revelation 15:3 (Moses is God's bond-servant)

So James is a "bond-servant". But whom does James serve as a bond-servant? Well, two Persons are named in the "Closing" to this letter (verse 1[a]). They are,

1. God
2. the Lord Jesus Christ

Person #1: God. The noun "God" identifies the *Trinity*. The word *Trinity* doesn't appear in the Bible, no, not even once. But the spiritual truth of what the word means is 100% pure, unadulterated Bible! The word *Trinity* is formed from the terms "tri"—meaning "3", as in "triangle" = 3 angles forming one shape—plus "unity" (i.e., the concept of "1" of something). So the noun *Trinity* portrays God as 3-in-1, or 3 Persons in 1 God (or 1 Godhead).

Brother James identifies himself as *a bond-servant of God*. His ministry is in the service of God, as in all three Persons of the Godhead (i.e., Father, Son, and Holy Spirit). During the Church Age believers comprise the Church, which is the Body of Christ on earth during this age. Ergo, as His Body we are directed by our Head, who is the Lord Jesus Christ.

However, in verse 1ª "God" is distinguished from "the Lord Jesus Christ". In this case we should view the identifier "God" as portraying the Father, the architect of the plan of salvation for sinners by grace through faith, apart from any works of the Law or man's laws. This affords us a fine segue into Point #2 of our list above, viz. "the Lord Jesus Christ", the third person of verse 1ª.

Person #2: the Lord Jesus Christ. Those three words are not a name, brothers and sisters. The first word is a title, the second a name, and the third a title. Think of it as being similar to, say, *President Trump*. "Trump" is his name, "President" his title.

The title "Christ" is a Greek *translation* of the Hebrew *Mashiach*. A Greek *transliteration* of the Hebrew word *Mashiach* is "Messias", which we *transliterate* into English as *Messiah*. The English word "Christ" is a *transliteration* of the Greek "Christos".

Confused enough yet? Not to fret. This list will visualize it for you.

1. Christ = English of the Greek *Christos*
2. Messiah = English of the Greek *Messias*
3. Messias = Greek for the Hebrew *Mashiach*
4. Mashiach = Hebrew for the English *Messiah*

Oh, but let us not be remiss and forget to define terminology for you. A *translation* replaces the Greek or Hebrew word with an English word which means the same thing. A *transliteration* keeps the Greek or Hebrew word, and replaces the letters of the foreign word with English letters which sound the same. Permit us to make use of another list for illustrative purposes:

1. *Christos*: drop the Greek "os" suffix and we have "Christ"
2. *Messias*: drop the Greek "s" suffix and add an English suffix "h", and we have "Messiah"
3. *Mashiach* means "anointed": *Christos* means anointed

Points #1-2 above are examples of *transliterations*. The original foreign word is kept and the letters replaced with similar-sounding English letters. Point #3 is a *translation*. The original Hebrew word (*Mashiach*) is replaced with a Greek work with the same meaning (*Christos*). Both words mean "anointed" or "anointed one".

The <u>name</u> *Jesus* is a *transliteration* of the Hebrew word *Yeshua* (Joshua). In Greek it is transliterated as *Iesous*. The name was revealed to Mary by the angel Gabriel, as God's name for His eternal Son when He took on human flesh and was born a Man. The name means "salvation of Yahveh". The word *Yahveh* is the Hebrew <u>name</u> of God, which God revealed to Moses at the burning bush on Mount Sinai.

The first word of Point #2 ("Lord") is essential for us to learn here, as it pertains to the phrase "Jesus Christ". This Person is also identified in the New Testament by the word *Lord*. This word is a <u>title</u>, not a name. It denotes Jesus as the King of all mankind, and also as the King of God's people, the believers who make up the Church.

The title *Christ*, contrariwise, portrays Jesus as the promised *seed of the woman* (Genesis 3:16). Man had just sinned, and forthwith the Lord God judged man as guilty and booted him out of the garden in the east. But before doing so, the Lord God promised man that He would provide him with a Savior from his sins, thus bringing God and man back together again in personal relationship.

Do you see from that information the significance of God naming His eternal Son in human flesh *Jesus*? Waddaya mean no? It's right there before your eyes. Look harder!

Okay. We'll point it out to you. The name *Jesus* means "salvation of Yahveh". The promised *seed of the woman* would "save God's people from their sins" (cf., Matthew 1:21). See the correlation now: "salvation of Yahveh" who will "save His people".

Whenever you see the name *Jesus* in the New Testament, recall that He is the promised *seed of the woman* in Genesis 3. He is the *Messiah* of Daniel 9. He is God's Savior from sins for whoever will receive Him as his sin offering. This has to do with Christ's first advent, the eternal Son of God's first coming to the earth as a human being. During this time He died on the cross and rose out of death to indeed save sinners from their sins.

Contrariwise, the title *Lord* as applied to Jesus denotes two of His ministries:

1. He is King of His people, the Church (the Church Age)
2. He is King of unbelievers (His 2nd Coming)

The Church Age began at Pentecost (cf., Acts 2), when the Holy Spirit birthed the Church into existence. The Church is the Body of Christ on earth during this age. The Church Age will come to an end at the Rapture, the moment Jesus comes in the clouds and stops there. From the clouds He calls out, *Come up here!*

Then all of the believers will rise from the earth to join Jesus in the clouds. At that very moment, every believer's physical body will be metamorphosed into a spiritual body, like Jesus Himself has been wearing since His own resurrection. We will return with Jesus to heaven to spend eternity there. The Church Age will be over, the day of grace, the time of salvation, a thing of the past.

Just as Messiah Jesus walked the earth in a human body and performed God's ministry on earth (cf., the Gospels), so too does He continue to do so during the Church Age. No, Jesus isn't walking the earth in human flesh today, in the sense that He did so during the period of the Gospel accounts. But yes, He does walk the earth in a human Body today during the Church Age. We His people comprise the Body of Christ on earth. Our Savior and King lives in us as our Head. We do His will on earth as His Body.

That much explicates Point #1 of our list above. As the Head of His Body, the Church, Jesus serves as our King. We serve Him as His subjects.

Once the Rapture occurs and the Church Age is in the rearview mirror of time, the Tribulation Period commences on the earth. This is the time when Satan possesses a human male, the antichrist. It is Satan's hour of fame, when he is allowed to play king of the earth and have his way. He wants to be God, does he? Well, then, this is his opportunity. It will be a bloodbath because Satan hates all humans and wants them dead. He cannot help himself. They are created in the image of God, and Satan loathes God.

The Tribulation Period will last for seven years. At its conclusion Jesus will again come in the clouds, only this time He won't stop there. He will come all the way to the earth, destroy Satan, and put an end to his evil machinations. This goes by the nomenclature of *Jesus' Second Coming*, as King of kings and Lord of lords.

That is how Jesus will be the King of every unbeliever, of all who refuse to willingly accept Him as their rightful King. *Kiss the Son, lest He become angry and you perish in the way* [Psalm 2:12].

Oh, but before we call it a day, let us refresh our memory vis-à-vis the identifiers of the God-Man as they appear in verse 1[a]. Simply press F5 on your mental keyboard, brothers and sisters.

Jesus = the actual <u>name</u> of the eternal Son of God, given to Him when He took upon real human flesh and became a true man. At that point in time He became the God-Man, fully God and fully Man in all aspects of His being. Prior to that moment in time, Jesus didn't exist. The eternal Son of God always exists, but the eternal Son of God in human flesh didn't. The eternal Son of God always is; the God-Man Jesus began at a specific moment in time.

Christ = a <u>title</u> of Jesus. It identifies His ministry of being the *seed of the woman* who fulfilled God's plan of salvation for sinners by grace through faith, apart from any works of the Law or man's laws. Jesus Christ did this during His first advent, the period covered by the Gospel accounts. Now that God's plan of salvation is fulfilled, Jesus Christ continues to offer it to sinners throughout the Church Age through His Body on earth, the Church.

In the phrase "the Lord Jesus Christ", His <u>title</u> "Lord" comes first. This emphasizes His ministry of being King. Recall that earlier we learned His kingship is twofold. During the Church Age He rules His people, the believers who make up the Church, the Body of Christ. As our Head, He directs the Body (i.e., us the believers). That is another way of saying He rules us.

After the Church Age Jesus is "Lord" over the unbelievers. He comes to earth a second time, conquers all who oppose Him, and rules the earth for a thousand years from His throne in Jerusalem (aka the Millennium). That is what a King (aka "Lord") does, you know.

So which ministry aspect of "Lord" applies in verse 1ᵃ of today's text? Well, James wrote to the Jewish believers of the 1ˢᵗ Century A.D., which was the Church Age. Ergo, aspect #1 applies. James is a bond-servant of Jesus during the Church Age, and Jesus is his "Lord". Let's hie off to the prayer closet to discuss this with Jesus.

James 1:1 (Part 2)

Yesterday we studied the "Closing" of the letter James wrote to believers. If you recall, back in the day what we call the "Closing" of a letter was used as the "Opening" (aka Salutation). If you need to brush up on this topic before proceeding in the text, retrace your steps to yesterday's study at this time. Go on. We'll wait for you…

Welcome back. Now we can commence with our exposition of the Salutation, or Opening, of James' letter. Let's read it together:

To the twelve tribes who are dispersed abroad: Greetings (verse 1[b]).

As we observed in our last study, that is the equivalent of "Dear sirs" in today's letters. If we follow today's paradigm for letters, James would've written,

To the twelve tribes who are dispersed abroad: Greetings (verse 1[b]).

Consider it all joy, my brethren…from death and will cover a multitude of sins (James 1:2-5:20).

James, a bond-servant of God and of the Lord Jesus Christ (verse 1[a]).

Are we not right? Yes, we are. That is the format a letter takes today. But format notwithstanding, this is still a letter written in the 1st Century A.D., for format doth not a letter make.

Now back to our analysis of the Salutation of this letter. It is indisputable fact that the phrase "the twelve tribes" is a reference to the Jews. No respectable Jew would be caught dead identifying Gentiles as "the twelve tribes"! It's that simple. Period.

There is this cult which teaches that Anglo-Saxons are the ten lost tribes of Israel. This refers to Northern Israel under the divided kingdom after King Solomon's death. The Assyrians conquered them and dispatched them into other lands of the Middle East, as it is recorded in *Tanakh* (aka the Old Testament).

In Great Britain this teaching is known as *Anglo-Israelism*. In the USA it goes by the name *Worldwide Church of God*, founded by Herbert W. Armstrong. To hear them tell it, those ten "lost" tribes migrated to Western Europe and onward to the British Isles. In time they wound up in North America. Ladies and gentlemen, let me introduce to you the Anglo-Saxon peoples, the genetic heirs of the Abrahamic Covenant.

Not! Beware this cult, for a cult it surely is. A cult claims to adhere to the Bible's version of Jesus as the Messiah. This identifies them, by their reckoning at least, as "Christian". But a cult separates itself from Christianity by exalting a "Jesus" of their own making. This is distinguished from a "false religion" in that a false religion doesn't claim to believe the Bible, but simply makes up its own ideas about God and all else relating to Him.

Let us be clear about this, brothers and sisters. The ten tribes of Northern Israel are not "lost". Even if man doesn't know who or where they are today, God does! And that's all that matters. At Jesus' 2nd Coming, He will call together all twelve tribes of Israel (aka the Israelites); and they will serve Him in Israel and Jerusalem during the Millennium as His chosen people. The Gentiles (aka the rest of humanity) will go up to Jerusalem to worship King Jesus on His throne in the temple there.

James, Jesus' half-brother, was a most respectable Jew. He would never consider the Gentiles of his day as the true Israelites, and not because of conceit, mind you, but because of the Word of God.

God made the Abrahamic Covenant with Abraham. To do so, God began by creating a new nation (the Israelites) out of one person (Abraham). This <u>separated</u> Abraham and his descendants (the Jews) from all the other peoples of the world (the Gentiles). We know this spiritual truth by the title *Doctrine of Separation*. God is separate from all of His creation, so those who would be a part of God's Family must be separate also.

By the false teachings of the cult we noted above, the Gentiles suddenly were mixed in with the Jews and saluted as the true heirs of the Abrahamic Covenant. Talk about cockamamie poppycock! You can't make this stuff up.

The phrase "the twelve tribes" = the Jewish people. They began as Abraham, continued as Isaac, followed by Jacob who was renamed Israel by God, who had twelve sons. These twelve sons grew into twelve tribes. It is really that simple, brothers and sisters. That is pure Bible with no cultic adulteration.

But leave it to sinful man to add to God's Word and turn the Gentiles into "the twelve tribes"! Astounding how we sinners cannot just believe the Bible. No, we can't restrain ourselves. Let us at it. We must needs change the Bible to its opposite, and thereby lead other sinners into the pit of hell with us. Flee this spiritual harlotry! The Church never (as in not ever) replaced Israel. Israel is Israel and the Church is the Church.

What are we to make of the clause in verse 1[b], "who are dispersed abroad"? The literal Greek text reads, *to the twelve tribes who in the diaspora*—with the verb of being "are" understood, as is customary in Biblical Greek. Biblical Hebrews regularly left out verbs of being because these verbs were understood. That was simply the way they talked and wrote, so it was second nature to understand them without actually writing them down.

And yes, we know that the New Testament was originally written in Greek, not Hebrew. But the issue isn't the language: the folks doing the writing is! They were Hebrews, so they thought and spoke and wrote as Hebrews were wont to do back in the day. So they habitually omitted verbs of being from their verbal and written colloquies.

Anyway, back to the phrase "dispersed abroad" (*diaspora* in the Greek). We didn't translate it in our literal translation two paragraphs prior, which makes it a *transliteration*—i.e., a Greek word which is written with English letters which sound like the Greek letters. It is used today for the location of any Jew not living inside the national boundaries of Israel.

This Greek word is a noun which is translated "dispersion". It is made up of the Greek preposition *dia* (through) + the Greek verb *speiro* (to sow) = "to sow (i.e., scatter seed) through" the nations. The Jews were the seed. Because of God's judgment on them for following the gods of the Gentiles, He sowed them as seed throughout the nations of the world (aka the Gentiles).

This Greek noun is used three times in the New Testament, with one of them being right here in verse 1 of our text for today. Let's read the other two together now:

> *The Jews then said to one another, "Where does this man (i.e., Jesus—R.G.) intend to go that we will not find Him? He is not intending to go to <u>the</u> <u>Dispersion</u> among the Greeks, and teach the Greeks, is He?* [John 7: 35, NASB]

> *Peter…To those…<u>scattered</u> <u>throughout</u> Pontus, Galatia, Cappadocia, Asia, and Bithynia* [1 Peter 1:1].

We underlined the applicable words under consideration. In the original Greek text they are the Greek noun *diaspora*.

We emphasize this for a purpose, brother and sisters. First of all, the Greek noun bespeaks the Jews of New Testament time who lived outside the Promised Land. Secondly, it is still used today with the same meaning for our time. All of this taken together speaks loudly and clearly to James' intention in verse 1^b: the twelve tribes in the Dispersion = the Jews of all of the twelve tribes; but the Gentiles are most definitely not included!

Greetings. This word concludes verse 1^b in our translation. The original Scriptures, both Old and New Testaments, had no chapter and verse divisions in them—nor any section divisions—so the division between verses 1 & 2 are irrelevant to the Holy Spirit. Sinful man thought to improve the Bible circa 900-1100 A.D., by adding these divisions to the text. Hence they ae not inspired by God. Consequently, we must never (as in not ever) hire a single one of these characters to interpret the Bible for us.

We don't say this to fill up space on the pages of this book. It holds great significance in Bible study today. We give the name *Proof-text Method* of Bible study to the most common approach used nowadays. A pastor or other learned believer proclaims to the sheep a doctrine acceptable to their church or denomination. Then he "proves" it is Bible truth by quoting a single verse, or even a single phrase or word, from the Bible. To them they just "proved" their doctrine to be spiritual truth.

Yea, about that… There are no chapters or verses in the true Bible, so that approach is fallacious right out of the gate! Understanding the spiritual truth of the Bible is achieved in only one way. We have to,

> *Establish a spiritual regimen of daily quiet time alone with Jesus, Bible open and man's books closed, with hands folded in prayer.*

If we put that spiritual regimen to work in our lives, we will be the blessed people of God indeed. If not, we will at best be churched and know some Bible facts in our head, even be sincere as all get-out about them, and think that makes us spiritual. But spiritual life requires the head knowledge to be copied by the Holy Spirit into our heart. There it grows the new life of Christ in us, the hope of glory. That is what it means to be *conformed to the image of Jesus*, brothers and sisters.

The above analysis does not have to do with *justification*. It is about *sanctification*. There are three aspects to God's plan of salvation for sinners by grace through faith, apart from any works of the Law or man's laws. The three are,

1. justification
2. sanctification
3. glorification

Point #1: justification. The word *justify* is a legal term. Imagine a judge sitting at his judge's bench and hearing evidence pro and con about the defendant. After the evidence is presented, the judge pounds his gavel on the bench and bellows, "Not guilty!" That is what *justification* means (cf., Romans 5:1).

A sinner comes to Judge Jesus, confesses his guilt (i.e., sin) to Him, and begs the court's forgiveness. Judge Jesus declares, "Not guilty!" But wait! How can a righteous Judge listen to the defendant unequivocally confess his guilt, and still declare him not guilty? Answer: because this particular Judge already paid the penalty for this sinner's crimes (i.e., sins). Consequently, there was no more guilt for which to find him guilty.

That is *justification*, brothers and sisters. It occurs the moment a sinner goes to Jesus as per the above example. That is what it means to be "born again". The sinner not only receives forgiveness for his sins, but also a new life of righteousness, God's own life in him, by which to refrain from sinning any longer.

Oh, but we are stepping across the boundary of *justification* and entering the domain of *sanctification* now. So let's move on to the second aspect of God's plan of salvation for sinners.

Point #2: sanctification. This concept has to do with spiritually maturing into the image of Jesus. Just as a newborn child has full humanity in him, so too does a reborn believer have the fullness of God's new nature in him.

But if left all alone, a baby in a crib doesn't automatically mature into a sound and healthy adult. The baby needs to be fed milk at first, and gradually weaned off the milk and onto solid food. In addition to that physical aspect of growing up, the baby needs to be reared to understand right and wrong, and how to deport himself in society as he interacts with others.

The same applies to the reborn baby. He needs to feed on the spiritual milk of God's Word (cf., 1 Peter 2:2). But as it is with the naturally-born baby, who requires to be weaned from a diet of only milk, so is it with the spiritually reborn baby. He needs to be weaned from his diet of only the spiritual milk of God's Word, and reared to where he feeds on the solid meat of God's Word (cf., Hebrews 5:12-14).

This process of spiritual maturity goes by the name *sanctification*. It begins at the moment a sinner is born again as a child of God. It continues through his entire life on this earth. Little to no spiritual growth (aka *sanctification*) results in malnourished saints with stunted spiritual life operating in them. Who would want that?

Point #3: glorification. This aspect of God's plan of salvation for sinners denotes the moment when Jesus returns in the clouds…and stops there! From the clouds He calls in a voice like a trumpet, *Come up here!* Instantaneously everyone who is born again, both the physically living and the dead, rises up from the earth to meet Jesus in the clouds. Jesus, then, takes us home with Him to meet His (and our) Father, the Groom introducing the Bride to dear old Dad. The Marriage Supper of the Lamb follows…and it lasts for seven years! And what wedding gifts (the believers' rewards) will be given out there too!

At the very instance when we believers respond to Jesus' voice from the clouds and begin to rise to meet Him, our physical bodies we be metamorphosed into spiritual bodies. These will be like Jesus has been wearing since His own resurrection out of death. That, brothers and sisters, is our *glorification.*

The first two aspects, *justification* and *sanctification*, occur with all newborn babies. These babies aren't partly human and have to become fully human before they are mature. Maturity consists of a growing process, which these babies experience for the entirety of their life on earth.

The final aspect, *glorification*, has no equivalent in the natural realm. The reborn child of God has already died on the cross "in Christ", so he enjoys the third aspect (*glorification*). Alas, but for the impenitent sinner, the scenario is not such a pleasant one. He dies physically (the first death), and then must remain spiritually dead for all eternity (i.e., permanently separated from God forever, i.e., the second death). He has no glorification.

Now that we understand these three aspects of God's plan of salvation for sinners, we are equipped to continue with the last word of verse 1, viz., *Greetings.* There are two details to muse upon vis-a-vis this word. First, it better fits with what follows in the text. Secondly, the Greek word and its meaning is of import.

Detail #1: where the word "greetings" best fits in the text. From our explication of the source of chapter and verse divisions in the Bible, we understand that the Holy Spirit didn't separate the text at verse 2 in our Bible. Man did that mischief all on his own—even though God severely scolds His people not to add to or subtract from His Word (Deuteronomy 4:2; Revelation 22:19).

We've already vetted verse 1; so we see how the verse serves as the "Closing" and "Opening" (aka *Salutation*) of this letter from James. But the word "greetings" is a part of the "Body" of a letter. This places it in what follows (i.e., verse 2).

Detail #2: the Greek word and its meaning. This word is *chairo*. It is a verb form of *charis*, the standard the New Testament Greek noun generally translated "grace", as in the grace of God.

The Scriptural concept of "grace" is "favor", as in receiving what we haven't earned and don't deserve. Oftentimes we read in religious articles and commentaries, that grace means "a free gift". No doubt you yourself heard it put that way.

Let us ask you, when was the last time you received a birthday or Christmas gift, and the bill for it was inside the box with your gift? Been a while, eh? Yea, me too. A "gift" is by definition free. If it cost us anything, it's not a "gift". It's what we paid for (i.e., not free). So the definition "a free gift" is a redundancy, bona-fide needless repetition. Better it is to phrase it as God's gift to sinners freely given—though a "gift" by definition is "freely given"! But at least the word "freely" is detached from "gift". That's an improvement of sorts.

The Greek verb *chairo* means "to rejoice" or "to be glad". In the **context** of verses 1-2, it has the sense of an imperative. We could legitimately redo the syntax (i.e., the sentence structure) and place *chairo* at the start of the Salutation. It would then read thusly:

Greetings to the twelve tribes in the Diaspora!

Another alternative is to translate it as contemporary Greek does. If you were to visit Greece and pass a man or woman on the street, the appropriate response would be, *Chairetai!* You've just said "Hello" or "Hi" to them. That about sums up what Brother James means in his letter. To the believing Jews who lived outside the Promised Land back in the day, James began by saying "Hi!"

There is one other detail for us to address. It's such a tasty spiritual morsel, that we wouldn't want to rush through our study and miss out on its savory flavor. We speak of the Apostle Paul's form of Salutation in his letters. Following the "Closing" to his letters (which is today's "Opening"), Paul pretty much begins by saying something like, *Grace and peace to you.*

Note the word "grace" in Paul's form of Salutation. The Greek word is *charis* (cf., Romans 1:7), which we learned from verse 1 of today's text is a noun form of the Greek verb *chairo*. Both Paul and James welcome the believers with God's grace.

However, in Paul's case he adds God's "peace" as well. Hmm. Do you wonder why? Don't put on your nonplused face! We'll tell you why. It's because Paul went to the lands of the Gentiles, while James remained in Jerusalem to pastor the Jewish church there.

Oh, dear. We are out of time today, so we will have to wait for the morrow to proceed. But the good news is that we can now spend time alone with Jesus before beddy-bye. Let's do it. We'll race you to the prayer closet. Last one there is a rotten egg!

James 1:1-3

We are about to finish up our exposition of the "Closing" and "Salutation", of the letter from James to the Jewish believers living outside the Promised Land. Our last study concluded with us in the middle of the stream, with the stream being the distinction between the Apostle Paul's ministry and Pastor James' ministry. What say we get out of the stream pronto by concluding our vetting of this distinction.

When meeting up with someone back in the day, the Greek greeting was some form of the Greek word *charis*. We learned that this is still true today. Throughout the Roman Empire, the Greek language was the standard form for day-to-day social intercourse. Consequently, this Greek word was employed in greeting someone.

The Apostle Paul went to the Gentiles, so he employed a Greek form for greeting them. James stayed in the land of the Jews, so we should expect that he employed the Hebrew greeting, right? That would be a no, brothers and sisters. The reason is that James wrote his letter to believing Jews who lived in the lands of the Gentiles. Generally speaking, they would have known Greek; but Hebrew, not so much. Hence James' Greek greeting to them.

However, in Paul's case he conducted his apostolic ministry predominantly in the Gentile lands. Even so, the churches Paul planted in Gentile lands began with both Jews and Gentiles. So Paul employed both forms of greeting in his letters, to show that the Word of God in his letters applied to all believers, both Jews and Gentiles.

You are wondering about now what the Hebrew greeting was back in the day. Yes, you are! I heard you wonder it. Well, we'll tell you what it was. The Hebrew greeting was…(are you ready for it?)…was (here comes)…was *Shalom!* Truth be told, this is still the Hebrew greeting in Israel today. In fact the word *shalom* is used to say both "hello" and "goodbye" in Israel this very day.

The Hebrew word *shalom* is translated into English as "peace". Paul wrote his letters to believers saying, "God's free gift and His peace to y'all!" God's free gift of salvation brings with it His peace, you see.

But don't misunderstand. Paul didn't use the Hebrew word *shalom* in his letters. He wrote these letters in Greek, so the Greek word which is translated "peace" in English was used. This Greek word is *eirene.* The Greek goddess of peace was named *Eirene.* Our English word *irenic* (not to misconstrued as "ironic"!) has to do with "peaceful" situations.

Still, the language isn't the issue. The person doing the writing or speaking is. The Apostle Paul was 100% dyed-in-the-wool Jewish. He lived and breathed Jewish. He slept Jewish. His blood was even the color of Jewish! (Okay. We made that up. All human blood is the same color.)

But we digress. Let's get back to Paul's greeting in his letters. When he wrote "grace and peace" in Greek to the believers, he gave them their familiar Greek greeting, and added his familiar Jewish greeting to it. After all, the Church always has been, and always will be, comprised of both Jews and Gentiles. God always has His remnant, and the sons of Abraham are included in it.

When we get right down to it, the early Church was comprised of only Jews. The Gentiles were the late-comers. So historically we can pinpoint the Church which once was totally Jewish; but the opposite never existed, doesn't exist now, and never will exist either! A totally Gentile Church is a figment of the imagination of sinful man, not a spiritual truth of our God.

Believers have "peace <u>with</u> God" because of His salvation (cf., Romans 5:1). This identifies aspect #1 of God's salvation, viz., *justification*. Because we are born again as sons of God through faith "in Christ", we are His Family. We have ceased being rebels at war with Him (aka sinners), and have become sons of His who serve Him in the Family business (aka saints). Peace <u>with</u> God.

Now that we have been declared "not guilty" in God's court (aka *justified*), we believers enjoy the "peace <u>of</u> God" in our daily living (cf., Philippians 2:12-13). This identifies Aspect #2 of God's plan of salvation, viz., *sanctification*.

As good sons God, we spiritually mature into the image of Jesus. We imitate Him by serving our heavenly Father. To do so, we must needs continue to spiritually mature, so as to know our Father's will for our lives individually, personally; and then we carry out His will. We do our part in the Family business, you see.

Do you see how all of this fits together as the warp and woof of eternal life? Scripture is amazing! Feed on it, and then exercise it to grow your spiritual muscles.

Okay, teacher. This is all well and good. But what does Paul's form of greeting have to do with the Book of James? Tell me. I am in suspense!

Ah, and a right fine query you bring up, dear brother. It's like this. The greeting James employs in his letter identifies his audience. If he had written it to Jews in Israel, he would have greeted them with "shalom" (or in Greek "eirene"). Instead he greeted them with the Greek *chairo* ("grace"). This tells us that the letter's recipients were Jews ("the twelve tribes"), who predominantly spoke Greek.

Consider it all joy, my brethren, when you encounter various trials (verse 2).

We noted earlier that the "greeting" fits with the "Body" of this letter. Therefore, verse 2 (as it appears in our English Bible) isn't the start of the "Body" of the letter. The word "greetings" is. But seeing how we already expounded on the word "greetings", we will now move on with our exposition of the remainder of verse 2 (our version).

ATTENTION!!! Verse 2 is the <u>theme</u> of the entire letter. Each tidbit of the letter must be served with the gravy of verse 2, or we will find ourselves wandering aimlessly through a dry and barren wasteland of man's opinions. Folks will think that we are sailing the Meander River! As we make our way through this letter, we will with regularity remind you of its <u>theme</u>. This will keep the text in **context** at all times. As Rule #1 for Bible study teaches,

A text without a context is a pretext.

For instance, in verses 3-4, Pastor James notes how each believer faces,

1. "trials" to test his faith (verses 3-4)
2. "endurance" which grows out of his trials (verse 4)
3. "perfection" and "completion" which grows out of his endurance (verse 4)

How are we to rightly understand these spiritual truths, if we skip over (or forget) the theme of the letter (verse 2)? Uh, would you believe we won't. Rather, we will interpret them to mean whatever happens to come to our fancy at the moment.

But God has his plan for our lives always! The trials which we face in life are a part of His plan, not the devil's plan. We mustn't see the troubles we encounter in life as someone doing us wrong. We are to view them as God doing us right! James is refreshing the memories of the Jewish believers about what Jesus taught them.

These things I have spoken to you, so that <u>in Me</u> you may have peace. <u>In the world</u> you have tribulation, but take courage; I have overcome the world [John 16:33].

Take a gander at the two underlined prepositional phrases in that quotation. They form a stark contrast. On one hand is the believer being "in Christ", on the other the believer being "in the world". We are *heavenly citizens* by virtue of our being "in Christ". Simultaneously, we are *in earthly shoes* by virtue of our remaining "in the world" until Jesus promotes us to eternity.

Walking hand-in-hand with the above spiritual truths are two concomitant spiritual truths, one per each of our locations as noted above. Since we are "in Christ" ("in Me"), we have *peace <u>with</u> God*, which in turn allows us to enjoy the *peace <u>of</u> God*.

In our last study we learned that our *peace <u>with</u> God* has to do with being born again and so declared "not guilty" before Judge God's bench (i.e., *justification*). We also learned that the *peace <u>of</u> God* comes from our spiritually maturing into the image of Jesus during our time on earth after rebirth (i.e., *sanctification*).

Throughout this letter, Pastor James parrots his half-brother Jesus' words. As a good Jew, he doesn't turn to the right or to the left with God's Word. He doesn't add to it or subtract from it. He simply restates what Jesus taught in the Gospels. This letter is Jewish through and through, but it is so much more than that. It is *Torah* (aka the Law of Moses, the **type**) filtered through the lens of the New Testament (aka the Covenant of Grace, the **antitype**).

Reread John 16:33 as quoted above. Now compare it with James 1:2-4. Jesus states that He wants believers to enjoy "peace", even while in the world they are experiencing "tribulation". James sees Jesus' "peace" as occurring during trials (i.e., "tribulation"), as believers endure "testing" and become "perfect and complete".

This is why James began the Body of his letter with its <u>theme</u>:

Consider it all joy, my brethren, when you encounter various trials (verse 2).

Of itself that sentence is nonsensical. Aside from bedlamites, who else considers it "all joy" when he goes through "trials"? The two concepts are antonyms, not synonyms. Let's see: trials in the right hand, all joy in the left. See! Told you so. They don't balance out in the slightest. They just plain don't go together.

Well, that is true for the natural man, the one born only once and knows only the world. But that is not the people to whom Pastor James wrote this letter. He wrote it to Jewish believers, remember. We believers can, and are expected to, reckon our tribulation as "all joy" because by means of tribulation we… Oops! The answer is to be found in verses 3-4, and we are still on verse 2. So we will get to the answer in a bit. For now let's finish our swim in the pool of verse 2.

Consider it all joy. The literal Greek reads, *All joy reckon it*. All joy comes first, giving it the emphasis. And it is not simply "joy" but "all joy". The more he spiritually matures into the image of Jesus, the more the believer recognizes all of life is God's work, His will for us.

And God's plan is never wrong for us. He always knows what is best for each person. The problem arises when any person thinks he knows better than God what is good for him! Walking in the flesh (i.e., making one's own decisions and doing what seems right in his own eyes) makes a believer to be indistinguishable from the unbeliever.

But the <u>theme</u> of this letter (verse 2) is believers ("my brethren"), the tribulation they encounter ("various trials"), and the proper response they are to have to it ("all joy"). Reread this <u>theme</u> several times. It is the foundation on which the remainder of the *Book of James* is built. No house can exist in one location, while its foundation is situated elsewhere! Or as Rule #1 for Bible study states the matter,

A text without a context is a pretext.

"All joy" is the emphasis, and it is to occur while experiencing "various trials" in life. During such times the believer's response is expected to be "all joy". Even more, King Jesus expects this of us believers because He furnishes us with the spiritual power to respond in such a way. Our power = the Holy Spirit inside us, who reminds us of the Word of God. This Word includes verses 2-4 of our text for today.

The Greek word translated "trials" in verse 2 is *peirasmos*. It is also translated as "test" and "temptation". The **context** determines which word to use. This issue is of import because of a misunderstanding which seems to stalk Christian Bible studies. We will encounter this sinister fiend when we vet verses 13-14. Let us leave it alone for now, and take it up then. Suffice it to say for now, that the same Greek word is used for both "test" and "tempt". Those two words do not necessarily distinguish good vs. bad.

We have one last detail to attend to, before exiting verse 2 and entering verse 3. The Greek word translated "brethren"—or "brothers", singular or plural—is *adelphos*. The word is used to identify all of us who are "sons of God" by grace through faith "in Christ" as our sin offering. This entails those who have been born again. Seeing how we are "sons" together in God's Family, this makes us "brothers".

...knowing that the testing of your faith produces endurance (verse 3).

Thus far in the letter James has called attention to the persecution, to which the Jewish believers were subjected in the lands of the Gentiles. Pastor James labels this persecution *peirasmos*. In the world believers <u>will</u> have tribulation of various kinds, ranging in intensity from temptation to trials, even to full-scale persecution and martyrdom. The Greek word *peirasmos* has to do with being tested or tempted, one word for either of those concepts.

Jesus employed this word in the Lord's Prayer in the phrase, *Lead us not into <u>temptation</u>* (cf., Matthew 6:13). He used it in Gethsemane, when He exhorted His disciples to stay awake and pray, *that you may not enter into <u>temptation</u>* (cf., Matthew 26:41). It is a common Biblical Greek word for temptation, testing, trials, occurring 21 times in the New Testament.

During the time of the early Church, believers faced persecution with regularity. Even when the persecution subsided, it was only a temporary situation. The believers lived in a state of expectation for its reappearance at any moment.

Any sane person knows when he is persecuted. Pastor James wants the Jewish believers in Gentile lands to "know" what it is all about. The Greek word translated "know" in verse 3 is *ginosko*. It refers to knowledge acquired through personal experience. Is being subjected to persecution personal enough?! Yes, we believe it is.

From their personal experiences, these Jewish believers are to know all about God's purpose for allowing it in their lives. After all, God is always on His throne and in control of all things. As believers we must constantly be reminded of this spiritual truth because the tensive facts of life turn our attention away from God and onto the perils we face.

In early U.S. history there was a period known as the "Gold Rush". Folks desirous of having a wealthy living hied off to California.

Sounds like the same as today, doesn't it? The folks who served to epitomize this event were given the name "the 49ers". No, not the San Francisco football team! They borrowed the name from the gold prospectors in 1849.

Anyway, when a few of them discovered gold, they took it to town to have it inspected by an assayer. This fellow was a specialist in metallurgy, so he knew how to separate pure gold ore from fool's gold. He was like an FBI specialist today, who can spot counterfeit money from a mile away.

You are wondering about now what this has to do with our text for today, aren't you? Well, we'll tell you. In verse 3 the Greek word translated "testing" is *dokimion*. It has to do with the work of an assayer from 49er days. Pastor James exhorts the Jewish believers to understand the purpose of it. It doesn't mean that God is overpowered by Satan. Nor does it mean that they are no-good sinners who deserve what they have to endure.

What it does mean is that our King is assaying us, to determine how pure our gold is. In the Tabernacle/Tent of Meeting (aka ToM) of Old Testament times, gold symbolized heaven. King Jesus is fitting us for heaven via our trials and testing. He is assaying us so as to remove the impurities, thus leaving only the pure gold. That way we will fit right in when we get to heaven.

This assaying of the believers is spiritual work, brothers and sisters. And as we are wont to express the matter,

> *Nothing spiritual ever transpires apart from [1]the Word of God and [2]the Holy Spirit.*

In the **context** of the *Book of James*, his letter is the Word of God to these Jewish believers. They must needs learn God's will for their lives from it, as the Holy Spirit teaches it to them. Then they must put it into practice in their daily living, in the power of the Holy Spirit. That is what spiritual living is. Since it is spiritual, it requires both the Word of God and the Holy Spirit.

Man's ideas and opinions (aka man's words) don't filter into the equation of what is spiritual. Man's words consist of Sunday School booklets, doctrinal statements, commentaries, chit chat at the water cooler, and all else not the Bible. Only the Bible is God's Word. Only it is eternal and thus able to impart eternal life. This is the gist of Rule #2 for Bible study which teaches,

> *The Bible is our sole and final authority in all matters of faith and practice.*

Yes, our King has provided His people, the believers, with pastor-teachers, to equip us for the work of ministry to which the King assigns each of us personally (cf., Ephesians 4:11-12). But these teachers are not a replacement for the Word of God and the Holy Spirit. Their job consists of two fundamental duties:

1. feed believers the Word of God
2. teach them how to feed themselves with the Word of God

A pastor should yearn to accomplish this goal amongst his flock, so the King can send him to another flock to teach them these same two fundamental duties in his job description. Each believer on his part should regularly wrestle with the angel of the Lord until daybreak, refusing to give up until he receives the blessing of his King. This blessing is a heart to feed on the Word of God daily.

Feeding on Scripture does not consist of sampling the wares. There is no such critter as *Buffet Bible*. Spiritual young'uns cannot leave their vegetables, while pigging out on the desserts. Scripture presents us with both blessings and curses. If we don't learn both, we will wind up with the curses. What's the fun in that? Let's pray.

James 1:3-5

Today we will continue where we left off yesterday, viz., in verse 3. We delved into the concept of "testing", and discovered its familial relationship with the concept of "assaying".

We also learned that the same Greek word translated "testing" in our text for today has the definition "tempting" too. It is a fallacy to think that the New Testament defines "testing" as good and "tempting" as bad. If you studied the *Book of Hebrews* with us, you are aware of Hebrews 4:15 which teaches us that Jesus,

> *...has been tempted in all things as we are, yet without sin.*

Temptation isn't sin: failing to resist it is. Father Adam was tempted by the serpent (aka Satan) in the garden. This temptation addressed three areas:

1. the lust of the flesh
2. the lust of the eyes
3. the pride of life

We see each of those three in Genesis 3:6. The Apostle John also enumerates them in 1 John 2:16. Read those two passages and see. Now flip the page over to Matthew 4:1-11, and read the account of Jesus being tempted by Satan (the serpent) in the wilderness. Jesus experienced all three areas of temptation, the same three identified in Genesis 3 and 1 John 2. That is how Jesus was tempted "in all things as we are".

And yet Jesus was and is without sin. Temptation isn't sin. It is "testing" to assay the quality of our gold. Our gold is the heavenly new life in us. Is it in control, or is the old sinner still in charge?

Verse 3 of today's text speaks of *the testing of your faith*. Our faith is what the King allows to be "tested" (or "tempted"). Biblical faith comes from hearing the Word of Christ (cf., Romans 10:17). To have Biblical faith requires that we hear the Word of God. To grow in Biblical faith requires that we hear the Word of God.

Even more, we require the Holy Spirit to teach us the Word of God that we hear. We cannot simply "hear" it with our natural sense of hearing and think this suffices. Only the Spirit knows the mind of God (cf., 1 Corinthians 2:9-16). Study this Bible book with us. It is available at https://randyg555.wixsite.com/heavenly-citizens/shop.

We see from this that Biblical faith requires <u>both</u> the Word of God <u>and</u> the Holy Spirit. This is because Biblical faith is spiritual and,

> *Nothing spiritual ever transpires apart from [1]the Word of God and [2]the Holy Spirit.*

The believer's "gold" (aka heavenly things) = eternal life. In the believer this entails the Bible and the Holy Spirit. Additionally, it requires the believer's faith in the Word of God, as the Holy Spirit teaches it to him.

The "testing" James references in verse 3 denotes the faith of the believer being tested. The part which grows out of the actual Word of God is assayed and found to be gold. The part which grows from man's words…well, let's just say it is fool's gold and leave it at that. Let each believer examine self to determine how wealthy or poor he is. How much gold is in your coffers, O saint?

The first result from *the testing of your faith* is expected to be "endurance". The Greek word is *upomone*, from *upo* (under) + *meno* (to abide or remain) = "to abide under". The idea is that, while being (or abiding) "under" temptation (or testing), the believer's faith is to sustain him, so that he continues to abide.

The Greek word *katergozomai*, translated "produces", is in the present tense in verse 3. The sense is that the believer continuously abides (or remains) while being under temptation. He doesn't give in to it and fall <u>into</u> temptation, you see. He withstands the temptation and abides in faith while <u>under</u> it. That is the sense of the Greek verb translated "produces" being in the present tense. It is the believer's lifestyle, not an occasional victory.

> *And let endurance have its perfect result, so that you may*
> *be perfect and complete, lacking in nothing* (verse 4).

King Jesus allows (and even promotes) struggles in the life of a believer. These struggles of various sorts "test his faith". If the believer's faith is Biblical, he grows in endurance.

We learned that the Greek word for "endurance" in verse 3 is *upomone*, which means "to abide under". While he is "under" the struggles of life, he abides—which means he doesn't cave in under them but persists in his walk with King Jesus.

This is where we have traversed the territory of the *Book of James* thus far. It serves as the **context** for verse 4, which is where we find ourselves now. In keeping with Rule #1 for Bible study, we establish the context at every step of our journey through Scripture.

As our endurance grows—which visibly illustrates, for all to see, how our Biblical faith is growing—our endurance is enabled to have *a perfect result*. Someone is scratching her head about now in wonder, "What does that mean, teacher?"

Again with the wondering, y'all? Let's not wonder. Let's resort to Scripture and allow it to speak for itself...or rather, to speak for God. We begin with the Greek verb translated "let (endurance) have". It is a present tense imperative, which means first of all that it is a command, not a suggestion! Secondly, as present tense, the action is to be done continuously, not simply at church on a Sunday morn. A paraphrase of the message might read,

Habitually, daily, hold to your perseverance, O believer!

Yep, that about says it all methinks. The emphasis isn't on simply sitting back and allowing (or "letting") this to take place. It is a command for the believer to exert himself in making it so.

We are soldiers in the army of King Jesus, O believers. We are at war with the flesh, the world, and the devil. We don't sit back in our comfy recliner and watch Jesus make things happen in our life. We must be actively involved in all of it.

As our Head, Jesus is in charge; so we take our cue from Him and do His will, not our own will "for Jesus". But we are His Body, His mouth and hands…and feet too. Jesus makes the decisions and directs us, as a head does with its body. But the body must act upon what the head instructs it to do, if anything will ever be accomplished in its life.

We are reminded of the cute little plaque we picked up decades ago. It reads,

The world is made up of three kinds of people. There are those who make things happen, those who watch things happen, and those who wonder what happened!

If we had to do it all over again, we'd buy that plaque again in a jinute, and that's quicker than a minute. We can't speak for you, but we choose to be among those who make things happen. That is what verse 4 of today's text commands believers to do.

Let's review the spiritual truths we have learned in our study of the *Book of James* thus far. From all sorts of <u>struggles</u> in life, the believer comes to <u>know</u> <u>from</u> <u>experience</u>—as well as by the Word of God explaining it to him—that the King is <u>testing</u> <u>his</u> <u>faith</u> so that he can spiritually mature. The Lord God tested Father Adam the same way in the garden, to allow him to spiritually mature.

<u>Endurance</u> is the visible fruit of Biblical faith. The fruit is needed because Biblical faith cannot be seen. No fruit = no evidence of true Biblical faith.

Spiritual maturity comes from exercising our faith, brothers and sisters. Anyone who pampers self and has a soft lifestyle is a spiritual Caspar Milquetoast, not a powerful soldier in the army of the King. He believes in the Gospel of Affluence, not the Gospel of Jesus Christ. He enjoys pleasing self too much to please the King.

The believer must daily, continuously, exercise his faith (which cannot be seen), by persevering ("enduring") under the struggles of life. Doing this will bear the fruit of a "perfect result".

The Greek word translated "perfect" means "complete" or "full-grown". It fulfills its potential. God created each thing to do the purpose for which He created it. The more a thing (or a person) fulfills God's purpose for it, the more it is "perfect" (or perfected), and the more it is "complete" in fulfilling its potential.

This is what spiritual maturity is about, brothers and sisters. We believers are to learn King Jesus' will for our life individually, and we are to put it into action increasingly. This is a lifetime growth process known as *sanctification*. It began at rebirth and continues until we are promoted to eternity.

We are siblings in the Family of God, adopted sons. Our job is to learn the Family business and do our part as we work in His business. Our Father is in charge of the Family business, so He assigns each of us our job (aka our ministry).

As we perform our job for Father God, struggles will arise which hamper the doing of our job. If we whine about it, run home to daddy and bawl like crybabies, we are not "enduring". The more we do endure, the more we spiritually mature. The more we spiritually mature, the more "perfected" or "complete" we become. Our "endurance" has *a perfect result*, you see. We are fulfilling our spiritual potential, as we serve in the Family business.

So that you may be perfect and complete, lacking in nothing (verse 4). The plot thickens, as Sherlock was wont to tell Dr. Watson. King Jesus tests our faith, so that we can spiritually mature. As we, adults all know that life consists of struggles. If we give up, we never grow up. If we persevere ("endure"), we do grow up.

In terms of our spiritual maturity, our endurance leads to "a perfect result". We learned a bit earlier that the Greek word translated "perfect" (viz., *teleios*) means "complete" or "full-grown". We fulfill our potential when we become *teleios*.

That is God's purpose in rearing us to spiritual maturity, brothers and sisters. We learn this from the second half of verse 4, which we quoted two paragraphs prior. The Greek adjective translated "perfect" is a repeat of the same word in verse 4[a], viz., *teleios*. This clause in verse 4[a] begins "so that" or "in order that". It is the Greek conjunction *ina*.

A conjunction is the "junction" where what precedes it "meets together with" ("con") what follows it, and what follows results from ("*ina*") what precedes. Verse 4[a] precedes the conjunction, and verse 4[b] follows and results from verse 4[a].

Ergo, by his endurance during struggles in life, the believer allows God to accomplish <u>His</u> "perfect result" in his life (verse 4[a]) by means of that particular struggle. This results in the believer as a person becoming "perfect", or "perfected" (verse 4[b]).

But there is still more meat on them there bones. Mama says we are not to waste any food; so let's clean off our plate. Not only does the believer as a person become *teleios* as an entire person by means of verses 2-4[a], but he also becomes "complete". Hmm. What does that mean? Doesn't the concept of "perfect" also have the meaning "complete"?

You are on the ball, dear brother. That is correct. The two words can serve as synonyms….until they don't! In this case they are connected together in the same clause; so their distinctions are emphasized, not their similarities. Let's consider their distinctions then, and discover how they build upon each other.

We already learned two paragraphs prior that, in the **context** of verse 4[b], the Greek word translated "perfect" (*teleios*) refers to the whole person. Over the course of many struggles in life, in which God tests his faith, he accumulates (or builds upon) God's "perfect work" in him. This accumulation of spiritual bricks builds him into a "perfect" person in which the Holy Spirit dwells. Hence the emphasis is on the entire person into whom he spiritually matures.

The Greek word translated "complete" is *olokleros*, from *olos* (all, every, the whole) + *kleros* (a lot which is cast, like dice) = "all that results from casting the lot". In the context of verse 4[b], the issue is the believer's life as he spiritually matures into the image of Jesus.

Let's put the two Greek adjectives together and see what the Holy Spirit teaches by the phrase "perfect and complete". First, as being "perfect" (or "perfected") by enduring (or "persevering") through life's struggles, the believer becomes "perfected" as a whole person. And then to emphasize how complete this is, the Greek adjective *olokleros* adds that this includes "the whole" person, "all" of him in each and every "part". The first word "perfect" = the whole person, the second word "complete" = "in all his "parts".

Consequently, this "perfect and complete" believer is found to be *lacking in nothing*. Those final three words of verse 4[b], you see, simply define the phrase "perfect and complete": such a one lacks nothing. And isn't that what we just learned from our analysis of the phrase "perfect and complete". Yes, it is.

One more detail must needs be addressed, before we vacate the premises of verse 4 and move into verse 5. Rule #1 for Bible study is so important, that we should repeat it five times upon rising out of bed each morning, and five times again before laying us down to sleep each night. This rule teaches,

A text without a context is a pretext.

Why is this so important at this juncture of the text, you wonder? And there you go wondering again! It's like this. The concepts of "being perfect" and "being complete" don't occur in a vacuum. They have a **context** by which we must perforce understand them. So before we move on in the text, we are constrained to highlight their context once more.

In verses 2-4 we have studied the believer, as he goes through life's struggles and comes out of them "perfect and complete". Don't lose me now. Ask yourself the question, "Who and what is the issue again?" Answer: the "who" = a believer, the "what" = the process of him spiritually maturing, as he conducts his life on earth as a believer (aka *sanctification*).

Therefore, we must interpret "perfection" and "completeness" as qualities of a spiritually mature believer. We must <u>not</u> interpret them abstractly, as in a vacuum, to include anyone under any other conditions (i.e., the wrong context).

An unbeliever—or, for that matter, a believer walking in the flesh by seeking his own will in life—will not become "perfect and complete" by "enduring" (or persevering) through the struggles he faces in life. Pastor James is not writing a contemporary self-help book about how to succeed in life!

This is spiritual truth, so it applies to spiritual people as a guide for how to spiritually mature. No others need try to follow these prescriptions, in order to succeed in life. First be born again (aka *justification*); then come back and study the *Book of James*, to learn how to grow up as a believer (aka *sanctification*). A baby must first be born before he can grow up. Right?

> *But if any of you lacks wisdom, let him ask of God, who gives to all generously and without reproach, and it will be given to him* (verse 5).

Hello. Is anyone paying attention? Even though we just repeated Rule #1 for Bible study, it is imperative that we do so again at this juncture of the text. Verse 5 is so easily misconstrued by trying to understand it in the abstract, that we would be derelict not to repeat Rule #1 again right this instant. So don't just sit there gaping at each other. Repeat Rule #1 for Bible study!

> *A text without a context is a pretext.*

Good job. Now press F5 and refresh those noggins of yours, to recall the **context** we just established in verse 4. What is the context? Don't be bashful. Someone speak up. Yes, you, ma'am, the young lady on our right.

> *The context is a believer as he spiritually matures by persevering through the struggles God allows in his life.*

You ace the course, miss. We are elated to know that you are paying close attention to the details of this book. So we see that, first of all, verse 5 applies to BELIEVERS, not just to anyone who desires to be the epitome of wisdom and truth, as he takes his bows during the fanfare from the masses while he walks by them.

Secondly, it applies to a believer in the **context** of him spiritually maturing. Any believer who walks in the flesh, seeking to fulfill his own will for his life, need not apply at verse 5 of today's text.

Verse 5 calls on believers to spiritually mature. If any believer is confounded during the struggles in his life, so that he is nearly faint at how to press onward to spiritual maturity by means of them (i.e., to "endure"), then…

That is the context of verse 5, that and that alone. So we mustn't think that, when it is time to take a test at school, and we spent the night playing computer games instead of studying, all we need do is close our eyes and mutter a prayer like this: "Jesus, help!!! Give me the wisdom to know the answers to my test questions!"

Don't even think it. We guarantee you that your prayer will bounce off deaf ears in heaven. Even a school kid knows better. The way God helps such a one to spiritually mature is to allow him to flunk his test! That way he'll know better than to be a slouch. How do we know this? Answer: because as a dad that's what I would do.

Slouching is the opposite of "persevering". It is to not even try to succeed in his responsibilities. Everyone else might have to try really hard, but not him. He is Yankee Doodle Dandy! All he need do is stick a feather in his cap and that suffices for him.

Now let's continue with verse 5. On second thought, let's not and say we did. Time eludes us, and the darkness descends. So we will betake ourselves to the prayer closet now, for a time of refreshing in the presence of our Lord Jesus. On the morrow we will return and proceed in the text.

James 1:5-6

Yesterday we intended to continue with verse 5; but the sun set, which rained on our parade. This forced us to cease our study and hie off to be with Jesus a while—a good thing indeed, and a most wonderful way to respond to our struggle with disappointment. But that was yesterday and this is today. So let's continue with verse 5 now.

The verse begins, *But if any of you lacks wisdom…* Once more, think Rule #1 for Bible study and ask yourself, "What is the context here?" The **context** is not wisdom for any circumstances which anyone at all is facing. The context is a believer as he faces struggles in life, which God wants to use to test his faith. Only by the testing of our faith can the residual old life in us after rebirth be removed, and we become God's pure heavenly gold.

Therefore, the specific "wisdom" to which Pastor James directs our attention has to do with how to do God's will, when facing a specific struggle in life. We need to get on our knees and pray,

> *Lord Jesus, help! I am weighed down beyond ability to survive. I am at a loss for how to respond to this test You have allowed in my life. Give me wisdom for what You want me to do to accomplish Your purpose in it. Amen.*

God's purposes in it are no doubt manifold, dear believer. One of His purposes, though, is obvious. We just learned about it in our studies on verses 2-4, if you recall. His purpose for you is your *sanctification*. Based on your prayer in the prior paragraph, we suggest you are on your way to increasing in your *sanctification*.

The life of a spiritual person is conducted as he *walks by faith*, not by sight. The walk of sight does what seems logical and necessary at the time. We might phrase it, "Thus saith me!" The *walk of faith*, contrariwise, does what is right in God's eyes. He reveals it to us in His Word, the Bible. The *walk of sight* phrases the answer, "Thus saith the Lord!" In terms of verse 5 in today's text, that is the true meaning of "wisdom".

There is an abrupt shift in audience between verses 2-4 and verse 5. As we've seen, verses 2-4 paint the portrait of a believer who is spiritually mature. He is walking in the Spirit because he has learned that life's struggles are used by God to test his faith.

This being the case, he cooperates with God, so that God can bring out of his life what God wants to accomplish in it. God's desire is that he endure in his trials and allow God's perfect result to be the fruit of his holy living. That much appears in verses 2-4.

Suddenly at verse 5 this changes. No, the subject doesn't become the unbeliever; nor is it per se a believer who is walking in the flesh. That isn't the abrupt shift which appears in the text. Rather, it is a shift <u>from</u> instruction about how to spiritually mature into a disciple, <u>to</u> instruction for what to do when confusion and lack of endurance occur during the struggles of life.

This is of great import, brothers and sisters. Sometimes folks come to church service on Sunday morns and think that, because they see the same thing week after week, it must be what "true church" is.

Included in this ritualistic approach is the big smiles on many folks' faces, which evoke envy in the Cheshire Cat. What with the accompanying school girl giggles and outward excitement and fun, why, some of the newer folks in the church service think such behaviors are the equivalent of spiritual maturity.

Consequently, when struggles arise in their life, and they don't yet know how King Jesus wants them to handle the situation, they get down on self for not being spiritual: "Woe is me! Will I ever be as spiritual as all the smiley faces in the church building?" These insecure folks aren't the ones we observe in verses 2-4, are they?

Indeed not! And that is why verse 5 follows verses 2-4. The verse begins with the Greek conjunction *de*, translated "but". It can just as well be translated "nevertheless" or "moreover". Let's employ "nevertheless" for the fun of it.

> *That is how a spiritually mature person comports himself (viz., as in verses 2-4). Nevertheless, should you encounter a situation in which you don't know what to do—and all of us have, or will, face such a situation—but if that is the case, then...*

Such is the gist of verse 5, brothers and sisters. The Apostle Paul has the same take on the matter as Pastor James does. Listen:

> *Brethren, I do not regard myself as having laid hold of it yet; but one thing I do: forgetting what lies behind and reaching forward to what lies ahead, I <u>press</u> <u>on</u> toward the goal for the prize of the upward call of God in Christ Jesus. Let us therefore, <u>as</u> <u>many</u> <u>as</u> <u>are</u> <u>perfect</u>, have this attitude; and if in anything you have a different attitude, God will reveal that also to you* [Philippians 3:13-15].

Mull over how Paul didn't always know the answers to every situation he encountered. He fell short at times, even after long years into his ministry. Still, he gave it to King Jesus and forgot about it. Then he got going again with performing his ministry work. Lastly he exhorted the young believers of Philippi to spiritually mature, so that they too would think and live this way.

Note the underlined words to that effect: *[1]I press on; [2]as many as are perfect.* At this stage of his new life "in Christ", Paul certainly was spiritually mature; as a consequence, he "pressed on" through his struggles. Using Pastor James' terminology, Paul "endured". Let the young believers in Philippi—"as many as are perfect"—face their struggles in the same way. The Greek adjective translated "perfect" is the same as that which occurs in verse 4 of today's text, viz., *teleios*. Not surprising since the Holy Spirit inspired both letters.

Anytime a believer encounters a situation he doesn't know how to handle as a believer—read, "if any of you lacks wisdom"—*let him ask of God.* Now why didn't we think of that? (lol)

Sadly, but the Holy Spirit wanted that said by James because it needed to be said. Consider how, the first time people encounter setbacks—whether believer or unbeliever, it matters not—but we have a penchant for growing faint and crying in our beer.

For the unbeliever, he is on his own. Sorry, neighbor; but Jesus does continue to hold out His hand to offer you deliverance from unbelief. Accept the offer, and you'll no longer be on your own.

The believer, contrariwise, is anything but on his own. He has the mind of Christ and the power of God inside him. The Holy Spirit is his daily companion and Comforter too. So how can he be on his own? The more he puts his position "in Christ" to use, the more he spiritually matures. The more he spiritually matures, the less often he lacks wisdom in life's struggles, those struggles which require him to ask God for needed wisdom.

Again, even spiritually mature believers don't know everything. As a good Father, God keeps us on our toes! He continues to allow struggles in our life to test our faith. This keeps us from thinking we know it all and don't need His help anymore.

The Church of Ephesus was a **type** of this spiritual anomaly back in the day. They knew it all, so they kept themselves busy "serving

Jesus". That would be "busy", as in "very busy". No, even busier than that! Why, they were so busy "serving Jesus" their own way, that they hadn't any time to spend alone with Jesus. Jesus labeled this spiritual malady, *You lost your first love* (cf., Revelation 2:4). Ouch! That had to hurt. Needless to say, but He wasn't much appreciative of their works which were done at His expense.

The Greek word translated "wisdom" is *sophia*, yep, just like the name. It occurs in some English words like, for example, *sophistry* and *sophomore*. Sophistry refers to specious reasoning, which runs counter to real wisdom. Sophomore comes from *sophos* (wise) + *moros* (fool or moron) = "a wise fool", i.e., a person who thinks he knows when he doesn't (cf., 1 Corinthians 8:2).

Let him ask of God. Can anyone say, "Prayer!"? When we need answers, we are to *ask of God*, i.e., we are to pray. Struggles in the life of a believer require *spiritual warfare* on our part. Read Ephesians 6:10-20 for a detailed account of *spiritual warfare*.

We must dress in the proper attire to conduct it, yes; but the attire, the armor, doth not *spiritual warfare* make. After putting on the armor, the Holy Spirit instructs the believer to PRAY! Prayer is the first step in conducting *spiritual warfare*. Otherwise the warfare is anything but spiritual. It is carnal, done in the sinful flesh. It is "serving Jesus", while being too busy to be alone with Jesus to learn His will about it—a symptom of having lost our first love.

Why should the believer *ask of God* for wisdom as to how to handle struggles in his life? Answer: because God,

...gives to all generously and without reproach (verse 5).

God isn't like the no-account dad, who's reaction to his son's request for help is, "Stop bothering me, you lazy kid!" That's not God! God "gives...without reproach". Ergo, don't fret asking Him for help because He will most assuredly provide the needed help. Oh, and He won't dole out the help with an eye dropper either. You can bet your booties, Granny, that His help will come in "generous" servings.

Think Joseph in Egypt, as he served his no-account older brothers their meal. They received food all right, but his younger brother Benjamin's portion was five times as much. We might say that Joseph gave help to his older brothers; but when it came to Benjamin, he gave help "generously". That is what we can expect from God, viz., that He'll give us His help generously.

The final clause in verse 5 teaches a deep spiritual truth. However, as Jesus taught in one of His parables, we believers won't learn it until we acquire a hunger for it, a hunger which spurs us on to seek it as treasure hunters digging for buried treasure (cf., Matthew 13:44). So let's not be remiss, but instead get to digging!

The hidden spiritual truth of the final clause in verse 5 is so palpable in its simplicity. The believer is to ask God for any wisdom he needs, *and it will be given him.*

Oh, no. There's your flummoxed face again. How can you not see the wonderful spiritual truth in that clause? Okay. Wipe your face free of that flummoxed look, and we'll spell it out for ya'.

The Greek verb is future tense, just as it is translated future tense in English. Not until a believer goes to God and asks for His help will he ever get it! That is the invaluable spiritual truth about which we marveled.

Eternal life begins on sinful man's part with Biblical <u>faith</u>. The fruit of Biblical faith is Biblical hope. Biblical hope drives the believer to search God's Word for the spiritual truths needed to live in a manner pleasing to God. Without Biblical hope, no one will search for spiritual truth as if searching for buried treasure. And without Biblical faith there can be no Biblical hope.

Now for the nitty gritty of this matter. Biblical faith is the opposite of natural eyesight. It is also not the same thing as intellectual and emotional understanding. Biblical faith sees what God sees because it is spiritual truth, not worldly wisdom.

We walk by faith and not by sight (cf., 2 Corinthians 5:7). This means we first obey God's Word, and then we actually know from the experience that it is true. It takes trust in God to live in such a manner. The **life tree** in the garden at the dawn of human history taught this very thing, viz., God's grace is received through faith.

In the same garden the **kogae tree** stood in contrast to the life tree. The kogae tree symbolized man thinking his own thoughts, and making his own decisions apart from God, as his way of life.

God said (i.e., His Word), *Eat fruit from the life tree, but don't eat fruit from the kogae tree.* By definition eating fruit from the life tree = obeying God's Word as man's way of life. By definition eating fruit from the kogae tree = disobeying God's Word, and substituting obedience to man's own words, as man's way of life.

It is no wonder that verse 5 follows the progression it takes. The believer first asks God for wisdom. Then at God's timing at some time <u>in</u> the <u>future</u>, God <u>will</u> <u>give</u> it to him. That is a lesson in how to *walk by faith and not by sight,* brothers and sisters. It was the very first lesson on spiritual truth in history. Father God taught it to His human son, Adam. It is kindergarten level. We can learn nothing else spiritual until we learn this elementary lesson.

> *But he must ask in faith without any doubting, for the one who doubts is like the surf of the sea, driven and tossed by the wind* (verse 6).

Verse 6 is chock-full of spiritual vitamins. Let's take our vitamins at this time, so that we grow strong and healthy spiritual lives. We will use a list to enumerate the spiritual vitamins:

1. but
2. he must ask
3. in faith
4. without any doubting

That much is the first half of verse 6. It is like the kitchen cabinet, wherein all the spiritual vitamins are stored. The second half of verse 6 serves as a warning label on each of the vitamin containers.

However, these warning labels are not like the usual warning labels, which caution against misuse or overuse of the product inside the container. Not at all! Instead, these warning labels sound an alarm about what will happen, should we not follow the Doctor's instructions for taking our vitamins. Let's not sit here gaping at one another. It's time to take our vitamins!

Vitamin #1: but. There is the familiar conjunction translated "but" again (Greek = *de*). In our last study we made his acquaintance. He served to introduce verse 5, if you recall. Waddaya mean you don't recall? Whew, boy. You folks must try to focus better. Here's a hint about the Greek word. It can also be translated "nevertheless". We experimented with that translation for verse 5. Good job. I saw the light bulb just come on over your head.

The context for verse 6 is verse 5. Really, it is. No fibbing. Verse 5 instructs a believer to ask God for wisdom. This believer is clueless about how to spiritually respond to a struggle which engulfs him. So verse 5 warns the believer, *Let him ask of God.*

The Greek verb translated "let (him) ask" is a present tense imperative, making it a command that must continuously be obeyed. It has the sense, "Continuously ask God until He gives you the answer." It is like Jacob at Peniel, as he wrestled with the angel until morning. Ol' Jacob wasn't about to let that angel go, no, not until He gave Jacob the wisdom he needed for doing God's will.

Vitamin #2: he must ask. This vitamin is another dose of the same vitamin which began verse 5. It is indispensable for interpreting verse 6. Hence the additional dosage here. By following verse 5, the opening word "but" in verse 6 cautions us to keep essential protocols in place, when we ask God for wisdom. This is apparent, if we take Vitamins #1 & #2 together: *but he must ask.*

Asking God = praying. Prayer is foundational for spiritual warfare. All else which is done in spiritual warfare must be built on the foundation of prayer. The foundation was laid in verse 5. What follows in verse 6 occurs on top of this foundation.

Let the needy believer "ask of God" (verse 5)…"but he must ask" (verse 6). In both cases the Greek verb for "ask" is the same word, and it is present tense imperative: "but he must continuously ask".

Fecund spiritual truth burgeons from these vitamins, brothers and sisters! The believer's struggles (aka "trials", "temptations", "tests") are used by God as stimulus for the believer's spiritual maturity. The believer's first response to any struggle is to be this: conduct spiritual warfare against it. This begins with prayer, continues with prayer, and concludes with prayer. He must keep on asking God, until he has victory over the struggle.

Oh, but there is more, much more, in the believer's arsenal for engaging in spiritual warfare. The believer may well pray about the struggle which is disrupting his routine. Still, all will be to no avail, should his prayer be focused on self and founded on fear. To avoid such a pitfall, the believer needs the rest of his vitamins. Let's go to the next vitamin container, then, and fetch it.

Vitamin #3: in faith. Without faith it is impossible to please God (cf., Hebrews 11:6). You would be well served to read the entire eleventh chapter of the *Book of Hebrews* at this time. It isn't known as the "Hall of Faith" for nothing! If you need help with it, we suggest you join our class on the *Book of Hebrews*. You will need your study book though; so go to our online bookstore for it, located at https://randyg555.wixsite.com/heavenly-citizens/shop.

This vitamin is often dispensed with, to the peril of the believer who does so. He returns from the battlefield—should he return at all—battered and shredded beyond recognition.

Even more often, a placebo is substituted for this vitamin. Such a scenario can be diagnosed correctly. It takes this appearance: the believer bows his head, mumbles a few words, and hops up with a swagger which portends bombastic undercurrents of the flesh. In fine, his prayer is not "in faith", certainly not Biblical faith.

Biblical faith comes from the Word of God (cf., Romans 10:17). To pray in faith (or "ask in faith") hasn't the meaning of bowing the head and telling God what we want, and then expecting his answer to be, "Anything you say, boss."

No! To pray "in faith" means that we feed on the Word of God daily, so that we learn to think like God thinks, and to see things from His perspective on His throne in eternity. In fine, we learn God's will for our life and come to understand His plan. We are adept at recognizing His hand, as it is at work in every struggle. And we want to do our part in the Family business to accomplish His will, not our own will. Ergo, we pray in that **context**.

Behold! the prayer of faith. It is praying for God's will to be done (cf., Matthew 6:9-10). Time is up for us now, so we will finish our vitamins in the next study. Let's pray about what we learned now.

James 1:6-9

Verse 6ª affords us four essential spiritual vitamins. We will not mature spiritually without taking them daily, even all day long! In our last study we learned about the first three; but then time eluded us, and we had to postpone descanting on the fourth spiritual vitamin. So let's do that now.

We begin by implementing Rule #1 for Bible study, which teaches,

> *A text without a context is a pretext.*

The **context** for the fourth spiritual vitamin is…(on your mark) is…(get set) is…(go!)…is Vitamins #1-3. In order to wisely handle struggles in life, the believer needs the wisdom of God (the **life tree**), not his own wit and wisdom (the **kogae tree**). How is he to acquire God's wisdom? Answer: *let him ask of God* (verse 5).

And that is where verse 6 knocks on the door and we let him in. Vitamin #1 is "but". Yes, we are to ask God for His wisdom for handling the struggles life throws at us. But… If we miss out on this first spiritual vitamin, we wind up bowing the head piously, muttering a few not-so-well-chosen words, and thinking we did what we are expected to do. We prayed, God. Where's Your wisdom? So as to avoid such a spectacle, the Holy Spirit inserts the first vitamin "but" here.

But he must ask…That is Vitamin #2. When "but" is able to get his attention, then "he must ask". Vitamin #2 repeats verse 5, which serves to connect it with verse 6. This makes it evident that instructions for how to pray ("ask") follow in verse 6.

In faith… That is Vitamin #3. "The typical approach to prayer is not acceptable, sir," says the Holy Spirit. If the believer considers his prayers, and he spots pious appearances and gurgling like a baby in the prayer closet, then he needs to give more thought to his prayers. Let him imitate Jesus' disciples, when they asked Him, *Lord, teach us to pray* (cf., Luke 11:1).

We will have opportunity to delve into the issue of prayer, as we advance through the *Book of James*. For our purposes at this stage of the text, let us realize that true Biblical prayer means actually talking to God, not just mumbling noises into the air. Scripture requires that praying must be done "in faith", which means we pray according to God's will as He reveals it to us in His Word.

This brings us to the last spiritual vitamin of verse 6ª, viz., Vitamin #4: without any doubting. The Greek verb translated "doubting" means "to vacillate or waver", and it is a present tense participle in our text. He must continuously be "without any doubting".

We are reminded of days long ago, when we spent our youth roaming the countryside and vast wooded properties. Grandpa and Grandma were from the country, and we were blessed to live with them all summer long, as well as weekends and school vacation times too.

Anyway, we rode our bicycles way off yonder along the country dirt roads, when we came upon a large pond down the incline off the road a ways. In the pond grew what we knew as "cattails". They were tall reeds with a solid top to them. This top was about eight inches in length and fatter than a thick cigar!

Here's the thing about this solid top. It felt like fur. When we roughly rubbed it in our hands, it broke apart into light and fluffy feathers of sorts, but much smaller than feathers. It was more like smaller pieces of feathers without any bone structure in it.

Well, we collected gobs of those cattails and took them home to Grandmama. She had us rub all the fur off the reeds and collect the fluff. Then she sewed a somewhat small pocket made of fabric, in which she deposited the fluff. Finally, she sewed this fabric pocket shut and gave it to us. Voilà! a pillow.

Here's the moral of the story, brothers and sisters. Those reeds, the cattails, were quite lightweight. Hence they blew back and forth in the wind, swaying at the slightest motion in the air. That is a fine pictorialization of the Greek word translated "doubting". A prayer not founded on the solid Rock of Scripture, well, let us just say it is "lightweight", like a cattail.

In verse 6[a] the concept of "doubting" serves as an antonym for the concept of "in faith". It serves to repeat the concept of "in faith", but as its negative. If we want to know the definition of a word or concept, we can learn a lot from and explanation of what it is not. Consider counterfeit money. To learn to recognize it, put it side-by-side with the Coca-Cola, er we meant with the real thing.

Such an approach was the norm with Biblical Hebrews. Their poetry followed this prescription with regularity. They "rhymed" ideas within lines, rather than rhyme words at the end of lines. Rhymed ideas which are similar are given the name *synonymous parallelism*. For dissimilar ideas it's *antonymous parallelism*.

In verse 6 we have a contrast, not a comparison. The concepts are dissimilar: "in faith" vs. "doubting"; so it is a case of *antonymous parallelism*.

As we noted in our last study, verse 6[b] does not contain any of the spiritual vitamins. Rather, it is attached to verse 6[a] as a warning label about the spiritual vitamins. Let's read it again and see how this is so:

> *...for the one who doubts is like the surf of the sea, driven and tossed by the wind* (verse 6[b]).

To borrow from our illustration a bit earlier in this study, we could translate it,

> *...for the one who doubts is like the cattails in the pond, driven and tossed by the wind.*

Methinks our translation is better (lol).

The spiritual vitamins build the believer up spiritually, so that he becomes a man of prayer, powerful in faith. The warning label then cautions him with the caveat,

> *But don't get caught up in a ritual in your prayer life. Prayer requires faith, which is the opposite of doubting. To have Biblical faith, you must feed your spirit; and the only spiritual food in existence is the Word of God. If your praying isn't founded on the Bible, then inevitably your struggles will grow the fruit of doubt in you. The result will be that you don't stand firm on Jesus, your Rock. Instead you are tossed about in life by your struggles, running around like a chicken with its head cut off!*

Such a scenario is sometime observed in believers today. The remedy for it is to be had from Biblical pastor-teachers, who are known for faithfully teaching the whole counsel of God to the flock. A straightforward presentation of this spiritual truth is to be found in Ephesians 4:11-16. Take a gander there and see.

> *For that man ought not to expect that he will receive anything from the Lord, being a double-minded man, unstable in all his ways* (verses 7-8).

The Greek verb translated "ought (not) to expect" is a present tense imperative. This makes it a command to be obeyed continuously. We might phrase it, "That man must continuously not suppose..."

Note well the makeup of this believer. As he tells God his troubles and cries for help, he has doubts in his heart. Huh? That does not compute. Can he really not trust God's character? Does he think God isn't strong enough to deliver him? Could God really not care about His own? Where does this doubt in the believer originate?

Oh, that's an easy question to answer. We just learned the answer in prior paragraphs. All of the prior paragraph is spelled d-o-u-b-t, DOUBT! We learned that the opposite of "doubt" is "faith". Ergo, the prior paragraph is the result of lack of Biblical faith.

What, then, is the remedy for the believer's doubt? Answer: more Bible. Really. We kid you not. It's that simple. Little Bible in = little Bible out. Lots of Bible in = lots of Bible out. No Bible in = no Bible out. Man's words in = man's words out.

So, let us stand in front of the mirror, and have a serious dialogue with the person looking back at us. Does he really trust God or not? How much Bible is he feeding himself daily? How much time, based on his Bible input, does he spend in the prayer closet praying daily?

What's that he says back at you? He says he is a very busy person and does not have time to spend in the prayer closet, or in the Bible either. Oh, really? Then does Dr. Jesus need go any further with him in diagnosing his condition of "doubtitis"?

If such a one really wants to cure his doubt, so that he can depend on God instead of on self, he already has his remedy in the four spiritual vitamins of verse 6^a; but let him be sure to heed the warning label of verse 6^b! He ignores it to his own peril.

> *And <u>without</u> <u>faith</u> it is impossible to please Him, for he who comes to God must believe that He is and that He is a rewarder of those who seek Him* [Hebrews 11:6].

That about does it with deciphering verse 7. Let's reread verse 8 together and tackle it now.

> *...being a double-minded man, unstable in all his ways* (verse 8).

The Greek word translated "double-minded" is *dipsuchos*, from *dis* or *duo* (two or twice) + *psuche* (breath or soul) = "two-souled". Note our English word "psyche" in the Greek word *psuche*. This makes our English word a *transliteration* and not a *translation*. A *translation* replaces the Greek word with an English word which means the same thing. A *transliteration* keeps the Greek word and changes the Greek letters to English letters which sound the same. Let's employ a bulleted list to illustrate this:

- ψυχή: *psuche* as a <u>transliteration</u> (our English word *psyche*)
- ψυχή: soul or breath as a <u>translation</u>

The Greek word translated "unstable" is *akatastatos*, from *a* (not) + *kata* (down) + *istemi* (to stand or set). *Kata* + *istemi* form the Greek word *kathistemi*, which means "to set down or set in place", or "to set over as an authority". Add the negative prefix *a* to it, and the word refers to someone who is not set in place.

This paints a picture of rebels who are against everything that is set in place or established. They are, in effect, anarchic, much like the rabble-rousers on our city streets today who burn and plunder and destroy because they want to get rid of this country and all forms of government...unless they get to be in charge, of course!

Such is a "believer" who doesn't quite "believe" God! He has two souls, you see. One soul supposedly "believes" God for salvation, but the other soul doesn't believe God to get him through his daily struggles. Like Jesus walking on the waves and Peter wanting to do so too: Jesus fares well and Peter is unstable because of his doubts.

But the brother of humble circumstances is to glory in his high position; and the rich man is to glory in his humiliation, because like flowering grass he will pass away (verses 9-10).

When it comes to interpreting Bible books, a problem which folks oftentimes face is that they don't apply Rule #1 for Bible study to the text. This rule is even more critical for books which follow the Oriental mode of reasoning throughout the book. James serves as a perfect example of this. So let us resort to Rule #1 at this juncture of the text:

A text without a context is a pretext.

The reason we raise this issue here is simple. For us Occidentals who are tuned to the Key of A (for Aristotle), Pastor James seems to say anything that comes to mind at the time. One moment his subject matter is prayer, the next moment it's faith, then works pop up… Woe is us! How can we follow his reasoning? Our Occidental heads start spinning, and where it stops nobody knows!

We don't intend to have this problem in our study of the *Book of James*, brothers and sisters. We don't say this because we are somehow superior to others. Rather, we have girded our spiritual loins with Rule #1 for Bible study, and we won't be shy in using it.

After getting past the "Closing" and "Salutation" of this letter, Brother James began the "Body" of the letter with this reference: *when you encounter various trials* (verse 2). At the time we studied verse 2, we exhorted you to fasten this reference to the frontal lobe of your cerebral cortex. We noted that it is the foundation on which the remainder of the letter is built.

In arriving at verses 9-10 of today's text, we passed through verses 2-8. At each step of the way we established the **context**; so we won't repeat all of it from verse 2 through verse 4. We will provide a brief overview of what we learned in verses 5-8, however. That will suffice to establish the **context** for verses 9-11.

Succinctly stated, verses 5-6ᵃ identify the *walk of faith*, and verses 6ᵇ-8 flip the coin to expose the *walk of sight*. At the very start of the Bible and the dawn of human history, this same spiritual truth was taught to the forebears of the human race, viz., Father Adam and Mother Eve.

Like a good Father teaching His infant children, the Lord God taught it by means of a picture story. (Though they were created full-grown, they still needed to mature mentally and spiritually.) The picture story consisted of two trees planted smack-dab in the center of the garden in the east. The two trees were,

- tree of life (aka the **life tree**)
- tree of the knowledge of good and evil (aka the **kogae tree**)

Eating fruit from the life tree was a good thing because the Lord God commanded our forebears to eat it. Hence the *walk of faith* = obedience to the Word of God. (Biblical faith = believing the Word of God in both the head and the heart, which results in obedience.) Eating fruit form the kogae tree was not a good thing because the Lord God forbade it. Hence the *walk of sight* = disobedience to the Word of God.

The spiritual truth was taught so simply, and yet so exquisitely, that even a small child could get it—which is who Adam and Eve were mentally and spiritually at the time of creation. Making this choice between the two trees served to allow them to exercise the *image of God* in them. God chooses, so those in His image do too.

In that context we are to interpret verses 9-11, which form one section of this letter. The foundation for this entire letter, once more = *when you encounter various trials* (verse 2). Verses 9-11 are a specific example of one of these trials, the first specific example, in fact, to be had from this letter. Many other specific examples follow in the remainder of the letter.

What specific trial appears in verses 9-11? Well, we must first confess that we misspoke. There is not only one type of struggle in life (aka trial, test, temptation) in these three verses; there are two. However, in our defense we plead the fifth—just kidding—we present relevant evidence: the two types of temptations are actually two sides of one coin. The two sides are,

- temptation from poverty & lack of status (verse 9)
- temptation from wealth and pride (verse 10)

That, brothers and sisters, is how verses 9-11 fit into this letter at this juncture of the text. (We will get to verse 11 after we vet verses 9-10.)

As we stated above, verses 9-10 are like the two sides of one coin. On one side we have *the brother of humble circumstances*, on the other *the rich man*. Ergo, by contrast we understand that the phrase "humble circumstances" is the opposite of being wealthy.

The Greek adjective translated "of humble circumstances" is *tapeinos*. It is used here as a masculine noun (aka a "substantive"). The word means "poor" or "humble" or "of low estate or humble means".

This poor man (compared to the rich man) is to focus his life as a heavenly citizen in earthly shoes. His natural life has died on the cross "in Christ". He is seeking a better country because he is a new creation "in Christ", a spiritual person now. His home is in heaven, not on the earth. That is to be his focus. As such, he is to *glory in his high position*, not bemoan his earthly low position.

The Greek word translated "glory" (or "boast") is a present tense imperative. This makes it a command which is to be done continuously in his life. Every single day until Jesus calls him home, the believer is not to focus on what wealth or status he doesn't have on this ball of dust we know as the earth. This dirt ball is passing away. As a believer he lives eternally, and in heaven with Jesus too! All of this and Jesus too: who has more than that? This is something of which we can, and should, always boast.

The person addressed in verse 9 is identified as "the brother". In the New Testament believers are identified as "brothers" or "brethren". This is the same thing as human beings being identified as "man" or "mankind". God created "man" to "let <u>them</u> rule" (cf., Genesis 1:26). Verse 27 goes on even more specifically:

> *God created <u>man</u> in His own image, in the image of God He created <u>him</u>; <u>male</u> <u>and</u> <u>female</u> He created <u>them</u>* [Genesis 1:27].

In the first half of verse 27 above, "man" and "him" (singular) are used. This means the "man" means "mankind" or "humanity", both male and female. In the second half of the verse, "male and female" and "them" are used. This means the reference is not to the collective "mankind", but to the individuals who comprise this collective.

In the same way believers under the Covenant of Grace are made one people "in Christ". We are all "brothers" or "brethren", a unity or collective which is comprised of male and female, rich and poor, Jew and Gentile.

Oh, dear. We are out of time today. Let's muse over what we learned in this study, while we enjoy the presence of the Lord Jesus with us in the prayer closet. See you again tomorrow, same time, same station.

James 1:9-12

We concluded our last study in the middle of the stream again, or in the middle of verse 9. Our flow of thought at the time was that believers under the Covenant of Grace are made one people "in Christ". We are all "brothers" or "brethren", a unity or collective which is comprised of male and female, rich and poor, Jew and Gentile. Let's take it from there.

When God referred to mankind as "man" instead of "woman", He never belittled females. When folks today want to change the Bible to read "brothers and sisters", every time the Greek word *adelphos* ("brother") is used for believers, it is faulty to the core for spiritually mature leaders to go along with it! We don't change the Bible to fit the world's viewpoints. We teach the Bible without adulteration to change the world's thinking.

Unbelievers *walk by sight*, functioning on the basis of appearance rather than essence. Believers are commanded to *walk by faith*. We are to function on the basis of faith, or on the basis of God's Word.

Unbelievers look at a believer's limited worldly resources and label him poor. By worldly thinking, being poor is the same as having very limited reasoning abilities, and very limited everything else worldly too! Believers, don't you dare fall into that trap! It is the *walk of sight*. It is to eat fruit from the **kogae tree**.

We believers must evaluate every person on the basis of his relationship with the Lord Jesus (or lack thereof). Believers are spiritually rich, eternally rich. It is the unbelievers who are poor, eternally poor. We have nothing to be ashamed of, unless it is how we don't value King Jesus highly enough.

We recognize this condition by how much of our time we give to Him, so as to be alone with Him and grow in our knowledge of who He is as a Person. If we do that daily, then our love for Him continuously grows. We maintain our first love. If we don't, our estimate of Him is reserved for the church building on a Sunday morn, and we value the things of the world overmuch.

As we noted earlier in this study, verses 9-10 are two forms of temptation which believers encounter throughout life. We also, noted that they are actually two sides of the same coin, which is also how the text presents them.

Yes, believers (as well as unbelievers) fall into one of two states of existence. On one hand are those with wealth, on the other those without wealth. But focusing on such a view of life is worldly. It is to *walk by sight*.

To *walk by faith*—i.e., to live spiritually, or to live in the Spirit—is to live on the basis of heaven. We are to store up treasure in heaven, not on earth (cf., Matthew 6:19-24). That is our focus. Jesus forcefully taught this truth in His Parable of the Talents (cf., Matthew 25:14-30). A "talent" in this parable refers to everything we have, not just money but time and abilities and family, etc.

At the Rapture, when Jesus comes again and takes us believers home with Him to heaven, we will be judged by Him at the *Bema*. This judgment won't be for salvation or damnation. After all, we are believers! No, but this judgment will be based on our works, in order to determine our rewards for serving Him.

That is the meaning of the Parable of the Talents, brothers and sisters. The entirety of our being and living will be weighed on the scales of His righteousness. How much did we truly love Him through the course of our life on earth?

The determination will be made on the basis of how much Jesus gave us individually. That is what we are accountable for. God gives every human being something, no, many things. He doesn't give them to us, so that we can feather our own nest and live the high life like worldly folks do. He gives them, all of them, to us, so that we can use them to build the Kingdom of God on earth.

Those with little money cannot give much money. Those with lots of money can give gobs of money! Forget this human, worldly measurement of money known as the "tithe". That was given to Israel, not to the Church. Israel was God's earthly people. They had an earthly kingdom with an earthly legal code (aka *Torah*, or the Law of Moses). Ergo, they were judged on the basis of how much money (and its equivalents back then) they gave to God.

The Israelites were required by Law to give the Lord one-tenth (aka the "tithe", a Hebrew word which means one-tenth). Truth be told, the Law required them to pay the tithe twice yearly, plus an additional tithe every third year. This adds up to an average annual tax of 23⅓% of their wealth.

The tithe = the taxes the Israelites paid to support their <u>earthly</u> government. We believers today pay ours to the federal, state, and local governments; and it's likely much higher than 23⅓%!

Do you see how verse 9 furnishes a graphic scenario of the poor believer facing temptation. Waddaya mean no? We'll have to start calling you Mr. Magoo! See an optometrist, why don'cha.

Imagine this poor believer, as he rubs shoulders with the rich believers in his church. He feels inferior because the world all around him promotes the rich and their wealth as superior. He bemoans his existence with the whimper, "Poor me. I'm poor." And his life never goes anywhere.

That, brothers and sisters, is the temptation of being poor by the world's standard. Falling for this temptation leaves the believer crippled. He never excels while living in this world because he sees man and man's standards, when all along, as a believer, he is to see King Jesus and His standards.

God gives _every_ person "talents". Every person is to use his specific talents to build the Kingdom of God. That is the scale on which each person will be weighed at the _Bema_. Let us stop whining about our lot in life, and instead get to work serving Jesus with the talents with which He furnishes us. Doing so will build confidence "in Christ", and a right eternal perception of self will grow out of it, and increasingly so the more we live for Him.

Having evaluated the worldly-poor believer, we have pretty much evaluated the worldly-rich believer too. The issue = where is our focus? Do we focus on this world and our lot in it? Or do we focus on eternity and our lot up there, and live accordingly?

If we see a worldly-rich man (perhaps we ourselves) and think of him as superior to the poor man, then we are _walking by sight_. If we see a worldly-poor man (perhaps we ourselves) and think of him as inferior to anyone else, then we are _walking by sight_. The _walk of faith_ sees each person on the basis of the Word of God, according to "thus saith the Lord". As the Apostle Paul put it:

> _Do not be conformed to this world, but be transformed by the renewing of your mind, so that you may prove what the will of God is, that which is good and acceptable and perfect_ [Romans 12:2].

That is about as clear and precise as the matter can be stated. Let's itemize the various contrasts:

1. do not be vs. but be
2. conformed to vs. transformed by
3. this world vs. the renewing of your mind

The purpose of ceasing to be an extension of the world, and instead become renewed in our thinking, is SO THAT. Huh? So that what, teacher? Answer: so that we will be equipped to know God's will for our life individually, that's what. Even more, once we <u>know</u> what it is, we will be able to <u>prove</u> it.

Huh? Again with the cryptic talk, teacher. Spit it out already. We are simple folk here. We need plain-speak.

Okay, it's like this. When we learn God's will for our life individually, and we put it into practice (i.e., we do it), the results "prove" it is true. Is that plain enough for you, brother?

Oh, and as one final encouragement for us to *prove what the will of God is*, the Holy Spirit promises that God's will is "good and acceptable and perfect" for us. Who wouldn't want that?

Let's finish our analysis of verse 10 now. We will begin by once more reading verse 10[b], so that it is fresh in our noggins.

...because like flowering grass he will pass away (verse 10[b]).

The poor believer is "poor" by the estimation of the world. He hasn't wealth, status, or any of the other things of import to those who see the world as their true home. The rich believer is "rich" by the estimation of the world. He does have wealth and status etc. In each case the folks in question are believers.

Worldly folks are expected to think and behave, based on *walking by sight*. They live for the things of the world because that is what they see.

But Pastor James wrote this letter to believers. It is expected of believers that they not *walk by sight* but *by faith*. Our citizenship is in heaven. The old sinner, that dyed-in-the-wool worldling, is dead on the cross "in Christ". Consequently, the born again new creation "in Christ" is to be ruled by his new life, the Holy Spirit in him.

This is the **context** for the spiritual truths incorporated in verses 9-11, brothers and sisters. The believer who is poor by the world's estimation has all the riches of the heavenlies at his disposal "in Christ". He is heavenly rich!

The believer who is rich by the world's estimation has died to the world "in Christ". Consequently, he lives the new life of Christ in him, the hope of glory, not the old life of the worldling who sees his wealth and status and thinks himself to be better than his worldly-poor brothers "in Christ".

The boast of the poor believer is that he is a child of the King and shares all the King's wealth and status with Him. The boast of the rich believer is that he isn't enslaved by his wealth and status, such that it defines him. Rather, he is a willing bond-servant of King Jesus. He gives Jesus all the glory and boasts of his elevation "in Christ", which lifts him out of slavery to the world and into the real wealth and status which comes by virtue of being "in Christ".

Both rich and poor believers are on the same level, you see, though each reaches that level from a different direction. The way they become believers is identical. It is by grace <u>through</u> <u>faith</u>, apart from any works of the Law or man's laws. This has to do with *justification*. What varies is the avenue they take in attaining spiritual maturity. This is about *sanctification*.

Part of the process in the rich believer's *renewing of the mind* entails his right estimation of worldly riches. He may well have them, though even worldly riches belong to King Jesus. He simply loaned them to the rich believer, and He expects the rich believer to put them to use in building the Kingdom of God on earth.

To function as a spiritual person according to the *renewing of the mind*, let the rich believer simply keep it fresh in his gray matter that, *like flowering grass, he will pass away* (verse 10^b). The reference is to Isaiah 40:6-8 (cf., 1 Peter 1:24-25).

Once more, believers are dead to the old sinner, whose life was tied down to the earth. The new of life is now inside the believer, and this life is our anchor within the veil of the Holy of holies in heaven (cf., Hebrews 6:17-20).

The rich believer is no longer founded on the world and its showy baubles. Such gewgaws *will pass away like flowering grass*! Rather, he is founded on Christ and His heavenly Kingdom, a Savior and King who never passes away, Who owns all of creation and eternity too.

Having preached the cure against carnality in the believer (verses 9-10), Pastor James adds one more exhortation to the believers against living for the world. Because of how deadly worldly living is to spiritual life, this repetition is proffered to the believers so as to emphasize the certainty of the matter (cf., Genesis 41:32). Let's read this encore performance together, shall we?

> *For the sun rises with a scorching wind and withers the grass; and its flower falls off and the beauty of its appearance is destroyed; so too the rich man in the midst of his pursuits will fade away* (verse 11).

The metaphor literally applies to reality in everyday life. Yes, grass and flowers come and go, and that right quickly! The moisture in the ground dissipates, the blazing sun rises in the sky, and the grass and flowers are gone in short order. That is a simple picture of reality, and it is applied to the rich man of the world. All of his wealth and status notwithstanding, he still falls into the category of "here today and gone tomorrow", just like the world's poor man.

And yet we cannot but see an eschatological application to the metaphor. When push comes to shove, at the end of days *the sun of righteousness will rise with healing in its wings* (cf., Malachi 4:2). This applies to believers, not to unbelievers. For the fate of unbelievers read Malachi 4:1, 3.

This eschatological application of the metaphor (verse 11 in today's text) recognizes the Lord Jesus as *the sun of righteousness*. At His 2nd Coming to the earth, He will deliver the nation of Israel from their unbelief, and establish them as His people on the earth. They will live in the Promised Land, and King Jesus will sit on His throne in Jerusalem and rule over them.

The rest of the nations of the world (aka the Gentiles) will either refuse to acknowledge Jesus as their King, or else receive Him as such. For those who reject Jesus as their King, He will crush them mercilessly as a rod crushes pottery, ridding the earth of them. For those who accept Jesus as their King, they will come to Jerusalem to worship Him in conjunction with the Jews. The Lord God will fulfill the Abrahamic Covenant during his thousand-year reign of King Jesus over the entire earth (aka the Millennium).

You would do well to reread verse 11 a couple of times. View it as a metaphor of literal sun and grass and flowers. Then consider it eschatologically, as applying to Jesus' 2nd Coming to the earth.

Oh, and please forgive us the oversight. Our failing memory forgot to define the word *eschatological* for you. The word comes from the Greek *eschatos* (last, as in "last days or times") + *logia* (words or teachings) = "teachings about the last days"—a little something extra at no additional charge, like a lagniappe.

The Greek word translated "sun" in verse 11 is *elios*. Add an initial "h" to it to compensate for the rough breathing mark which precedes the Greek word, and replace the Greek suffix "os" with the Latin suffix "ium", and voilà! our English word *helium*. It is no coincidence that the most abundant elements in the universe are hydrogen and helium, in that order. The sun is believed to be made up of 70% hydrogen and 28% helium.

We get our English word *helium* from the Greek word for "sun". This makes our English word a *transliteration*, not a *translation*. A *translation* replaces the Greek word with an English word which means the same thing. A *transliteration* keeps the Greek word and changes the Greek letters to English letters which sound the same.

The Greek verb translated "is destroyed" is *apollumi*. A noun form of this word is employed by the Apostle John in Revelation 9:11. Let's read it together:

> *They have as king over them, the angel of the abyss; his name in Hebrew is Abaddon, and in the Greek he has the name Apollyon* [Revelation 9:11].

As we can see in verse 11 of our text for today, the verb form of this word means "is destroyed". The noun form means "destroyer", as does the Hebrew word "Abaddon".

> *Blessed is a man who perseveres under trial; for once he has been approved, he will receive the crown of life which the Lord has promised to those who love Him* (verse 12).

Before we take one more step forward in the text, we must perforce reiterate Rule #1 for Bible study:

> *A text without a context is a pretext.*

This step is required at this juncture of the text because, without it, a wrong interpretation of verse 12 is often made. The topic is *a man who perseveres under trial*. That is as plain as the nose on our face, is it not? It is simply a literal quotation of a clause from the verse, with no additions for promoting an agenda.

The problem arises when the verse is taken out of **context**. This is done by applying it to any sort of "trial" (aka test or temptation). The spiritual truth taught in verse 11 may well fit with any test at all, but its application in verse 11 has a different context than that.

If we don't stick with the context, we have a pretext. That is a sad state of affairs to be in, when it comes time to apply the Bible to our daily living. It puts words in God's mouth, or more accurately in His Book. Man saying God says something doesn't make it so!

What, then, is the context for verse 12? As the famous secret agent Maxwell Smart would phrase the matter, "Would you believe…? Yes, would you believe the context is verses 9-11. Why, looky there, ma. I see verses 9-11! How'd they get there? We can tell that some of y'all are thinking that very thing. The blank stare on your faces is a dead giveaway.

Sorry, Charlie, but we are out of time today. But not to fret. We will be sure to deliver you from your blank stare in our next study. For the remainder of today, spend time alone with Jesus. Perhaps you won't have to wait for tomorrow. Jesus is known to deliver folks from blank stares. Ask Him to do so. He's the one who taught me to do it!

James 1:12

Our last study concluded in verse 12. We haven't come close to finishing the verse yet, so let's jump right into the deep end of the pool and attend to business. We will begin by rereading the verse.

> *Blessed is a man who perseveres under trial; for once he has been approved, he will receive the crown of life which the Lord has promised to those who love Him* (verse 12).

Verse 12 is not floating in space, unattached to anything else. It is directly connected with the temptation (aka the trial or test) which appears in verses 9-11. That trial, once more, is the temptation of depending on worldly wealth and status, rather than on Jesus. The temptation = to *walk by sight*, and call on God for help only when all else fails. The temptation is to view one's wealth and status as if Jesus is impressed by them, just because puny man is.

In terms of that specific temptation—and it is a whopper!—the Holy Spirit exults, *Blessed is the believer who perseveres under that temptation!* Jesus phrased the matter thusly, *How hard it is for a rich man to enter the kingdom of heaven!* [Matthew 19:23]

Folks who wallow in wealth tend to think they have everything under control; so they don't depend on God (i.e., have faith in Him) to lead them in life. The end result is that they *walk by sight*, not *by faith*. Houston, we have a problem!

God's salvation for sinners is by grace <u>through</u> <u>faith</u>. Without faith it is impossible to please God (cf., Hebrews 11:6). By depending on their riches, rich men are deficient in faith. This excludes them from God's plan of salvation. But praise the Lord! With God all things are possible. Ergo, some rich men do become born again. Thank you, Jesus!

Verse 12 affords us new insight into the person Pastor James. Take a gander at Matthew 5:1-12. Go ahead. We'll wait on y'all…

Good job. Glad to have you back. Now reread verse 12 of today's text. Do you see the family resemblance? Waddaya mean no? It's there. Look harder! (lol)

Pastor James is more than spiritual kin to King Jesus, members of the same spiritual family, the Church. Pastor James is also natural birth kin to Jesus. They are half-brothers. The erstwhile Jewish virgin, Miriam by name, was mama to both of them, though they had different fathers.

Joseph was James' father, the Holy Spirit Jesus'. James was conceived according to the natural order of things, Jesus supernaturally by the Holy Spirit coming upon Miriam. Spirits don't have bodies, so Miriam remained a virgin after Jesus' conception…though obviously not after James' conception.

In the same way God called all of creation into existence *ex nihilo* ("out of nothing"), so did He call into existence the sperm which grew into Jesus' human nature. Natural, physical means weren't employed. A miracle 'twas. A "miracle" is a deed which isn't accomplished by the natural order of things. Why would any believer find it hard to believe the Word of God's take on the birth of Jesus? God is in the business of working miracles, after all!

Five paragraphs prior we instructed you to read the *Beatitudes*, the name given to Matthew 5:1-12, which serves as the introduction to the Sermon on the Mount. The word *beatitudes* means "blessed".

Nine times in this introduction Jesus begins a different attitude with the word "blessed". Hence the name *beatitudes* is used for them. We direct you to focus on verses 10-12 of the *Beatitudes*, as a rather specific comparison with James 1:12.

The Greek adjective translated "blessed" is *makarios*. It means "blessed", which in turn means "happy" or "fortunate". In the New Testament the word denotes a believer being happy or fortunate, specifically because he is the recipient of God's divine favor. Any good thing which occurs in his life is the fruit of him having God's favor. Hence he is *makarios* (i.e., "blessed"). We see from this that the word is used in Scripture in a spiritual sense, and not simply as man enjoying the world and its goodies.

Early on in these studies in the *Book of James*, we noted that verse 2 is the theme of the book. Let's reread it to refresh our memory:

> *Consider it all joy, my brethren, when you encounter various <u>trials</u>* (verse 2).

As we learned back then, the underlined word in the Greek is *peirasmos*. The word is not just translated as "trials", but also as "tests" or "temptations". Well, this same Greek word is used in verse 12 of today's study.

Oh, but that is not the only connection to be had! Consider that the concept "consider it all joy" in verse 2 is the same thing as "blessed is a man" (i.e., "you are blessed, so consider it so"). This is a second specific connection between verses 2 and 12.

And there's more! Verse 3 follows this up with the reason why believers under persecution are to "consider it all joy" (verse 2):

> *...knowing that the testing of your faith produces <u>endurance</u>* (verse 3).

The underlined noun in the Greek is *upomone*, which we also studied back in verse 3. Would it surprise you to learn that the Greek verb translated "perseveres" in verse 12 is *upomeno*. Those are the same Greek words, except one is a noun, the other a verb.

That makes a grand total of three specific correlations between verse 12 and verses 2-3...three of those little buggers! Not exactly good odds for a coincidence.

Now let's put the cherry on top the sundae and enjoy the treat. Verse 4 follows verses 2-3 to make verses 2-4 a unified spiritual teaching. The verse identifies the outcome of a believer rejoicing under his struggles and persevering through them, which is this:

> *And let endurance have its perfect result, <u>so that</u> you may*
> *be perfect and complete, lacking in nothing* (verse 4).

Pay special attention to the underlined words in verse 4 as just quoted. The first half of verse 4 (preceding the underlined words) ties verse 4 to verses 2-3—which form only one sentence though they are broken down into two verses. Go figure. The second half of verse 4 then identifies the desired outcome for verses 2-3.

Reread it again, viz., the words following the underlined words, only read slowly, meditatively. No, even slower than that. That's better, but try it once more at a turtle's pace. Now read the second half of verse 12, the part following the semicolon. What's that you say? It's not clear enough for you? You demand plain-speak? Okay, then let's compare the two side-by-side, so to speak:

- <u>so</u> <u>that</u> you may be perfect and complete, lacking in nothing
- <u>for</u> <u>once</u> <u>he</u> <u>has</u> <u>been</u> <u>approved</u>, he will receive the crown of life which the Lord has promised to those who love Him

The underlined words in both comparisons have the same function, viz., to identify that what follows is the result of all that precedes it in verses 2-4[a] (as per the first bullet of our list above), and in verse 12[a] for the second bullet. What follows the underlined words is the same general spiritual truth: the result of living as spiritual men is spiritual completeness, which Jesus will reward at the *Bema*.

Think about it. Every believer, once he receives the crown of life from the Lord, <u>will</u> indubitably be "perfect and complete". That is indisputable! He <u>will</u> lack nothing whatsoever. Again, indubitable. See! The words following the underlined words, for each bullet of our bulleted list above, are synonymous. This is typical for the style of Biblical Hebrew poetry.

In verse 3 the Greek word translated "testing" is *dokimion*. In verse 12 the Greek word translated "approved" is…(wait for it) is…(do not be impatient) is *dokimos*. The noun *dokimion* is the root word of the adjective *dokimos*.

The noun *dokimion* denotes a "test" given to prove what is pure or genuine ore, while the adjective *dokimos* indicates the result of the "test", viz., that the ore "tested" is "approved" as being genuine or Coca-Cola, er, we mean the real thing.

Now let's apply this understanding to verse 12 of today's text. A person—in James' case a believer—who bears up under various temptations, and has been found to be genuine spiritual material by the tests, he shall receive the crown of life. As Sergeant Schultz was fond of phrasing the issue, *Very interesting*. Only you have to hear it in a thick German accent. But what does it all mean?

Don't you dare put on your nonplused face again! We'll give it to you in plain-speak. But first we will explain what it doesn't mean. This is necessary because our Arminian brethren—like some old heifers wading through the pond as they drink—have muddied the waters of spiritual truth on the subject.

Arminian doctrine teaches that believers can, and do, lose their salvation when they sin. In consequence they need to be born again all over—and presumably begin again at the beginning of spiritual life. Accordingly, Arminianism claims that believers must do good works to avoid sinning and stay saved.

This applies to verse 12 because they snatch hold of the phrase about first being tested, and only then will a believer receive the crown of life. To this our Arminian brethren rejoice:

Ah ha!. Told ya' so! To receive the crown of life requires a believer to be victorious over any and all temptations. So salvation is not by faith alone, but by faith plus the believer's good works!

Then they sit back down on their haunches, confident that they are the man as they relish the accolades of all their fawning acolytes.

Uh, not so fast there, amigo. You have failed to follow Rule #1 for Bible study, and in the doing of it stumbled over manmade doctrine and landed on your head in a ditch…a deep ditch at that! It will take a lot of work to clean up your mess. Nonetheless, somebody has to do it; so why not us? Let's get to it then.

First and foremost is the spiritual truth that Pastor James sent this letter to Jewish <u>believers</u>. Over and over again he speaks to them as *adelphos*, brethren. In the New Testament this is the word used of believers, unless the **context** specifically demands otherwise. Believers, and not unbelievers, are siblings in the Family of God. All of us are "brethren".

This being the case, the Holy Spirit doesn't instruct the believers how to be saved. They already are, which has to do with the issue of *justification*, the result of being born again.

Pastor James writes to the Jewish believers in the *diaspora*—the Gentile lands outside the Promised Land—about the necessity to spiritually mature into full-fledged disciples of King Jesus. His letter amounts to this: Grow up, y'all! Serve your King with your entire lives! This has to do with the issue of *sanctification*, spiritual maturity in the lives of believers, a process lasting through eternity.

Ergo, being born again isn't the issue in this letter. Nor is staying born again the issue. Living as born again 'tis.

"But why isn't staying born again the issue, teacher," a sweet soul queries. It's like this, ma'am. That issue is the prerogative of King Jesus and King Jesus alone. He alone judges the living and the dead to determine whether or not they are born again. This requires the ability to examine the heart, and no mere man can do so.

Consequently, it is none of any mere man's beeswax to dabble into the "what ifs" of spiritual truth. The only thing any human being can know about spiritual truth is what we can learn from God's Word, as the Holy Spirit teaches it to us. And seldom in the Bible are we told who is saved and who isn't. (Judas Iscariot wasn't.)

Believers are taught the requirements needed to be saved; and we are instructed to go into all the world and teach the folks these requirements, so that they too can be saved. But we are not the judges of salvation in anyone's life. We do not put anyone into heaven or hell. That is the prerogative of King Jesus alone. Beware encroaching on the rights of the King!

This is not to mention how we mere humans would only pull up the wheat with the weeds, putting saved folks in hell because they don't live up to the traditions of our church. And many an unsaved person would wind up in heaven by our reckoning too, because they know how to dot there i's and cross their t's when it comes to our church traditions. No doubt about it. We sure would make good judges concerning eternal matters! (Forgive us the sarcasm.)

As we already learned about verses 2-12 of this letter, the subject matter is how, as a believer, to respond to struggles in life. We begin by asking God for wisdom vis-à-vis the specific trial. "How, dear Jesus, am I to respond to it?" The improper prayer is, "How, dear Jesus, am I to stay saved in the midst of it?"

Jesus will hear our prayer and lead us to a proper response for the specific struggle. We will follow His leading in the power of the Spirit, with the result that we persevere. We will come out on the other end of Temptation Tunnel, with the realization that King Jesus used it to test our faith…and we passed! We <u>know</u> we passed for two reasons:

1. we persevered to the end of the temptation
2. we realize we passed

The realization that we passed the Lord's test requires spiritual maturity, and spiritual maturity is not to be found in apostasy (i.e., falling away from the Lord Jesus)!

The Greek word translated "apostasy" (cf., 2 Thessalonians 2:3) is *apostasia*, from *apo* (away from) + *istemi* (to stand) = "to stand away from". The sense is that the apostate once stood with King Jesus on the basis of His Word. But no longer! Now he stands away from the King by choosing to stand with man on the basis of man's words.

Sin is <u>always</u> a matter of choosing man's words (and usually one's own words) over God's Word. Consider that spiritual truth carefully, brothers and sisters. The apostate rejects God's Word. How then can he be saved? Salvation is *by grace through faith* (cf., Ephesians 2:8), and *faith comes from hearing the Word of Christ* (cf., Romans 10:17). Anyone who rejects God's Word about how to be saved, such a one is outside the realm of God's Kingdom.

And yet as we learned in prior paragraphs, no one can see the heart to decide who actually is saved or not, much less whether they then lost their salvation—or simply fell into sin, and need to flee to their city of refuge at 1 John 1:9. There they can confess their sins to Jesus, and He will put them through a thorough feet-washing (i.e., cover their sins with the blood of the Lamb; cf., John 13:1-17).

As Jesus taught Peter when He washed the disciples' feet, Peter didn't need to be washed all over. He already was (cf., John 13:5-11)! But he needed his feet washed again because walking the sinful earth in sinful flesh results in the believer falling into sin.

Take Apostle Peter himself. No sooner did Jesus finish washing his feet, than Peter denied three times that he even knew Jesus (cf., Matthew 26:69-75)! Talk about needing our feet washed!

But Peter didn't need to be washed all over again. He needed only to have his feet washed. The one-time event of being born again is portrayed in Scripture as being washed all over, as buried in death "in Christ" and rising out of death to new life "in Christ". Burial does not consist of having a portion of the body covered by dirt!

Believer's baptism employs the imagery of water as representing the dirt, as the ingredient which covers the lifeless corpse. Hence the need in water baptism to totally cover the participant in the water, in order to maintain the proper imagery.

However, the ritual of water baptism doesn't do the saving: it only serves as a visible physical reality of time and space, to pictorialize the invisible spiritual truth of dying and being buried "in Christ", and rising out of death to newness of life "in Christ".

Putting all of this spiritual truth together, we understand that Jesus' feet-washing served to teach two spiritual truths. Both of them are vital to understanding God's plan of salvation by grace through faith, apart from any works of the Law or man's laws. The two are,

1. salvation is portrayed as being washed all over
2. believer's confession and repentance = feet-washing

A believer still sins at times (cf., 1 John 1:8-10). He doesn't lose his salvation thereby and need to be born again (washed all over) and restart at the beginning (Point #1 above). He needs to confess his sins to Jesus and ask Him to wash his feet (Point #2 above).

Now let's return to verse 12 of today's text and finish vetting it. It will be our wisdom to reread the verse before doing so:

> *Blessed is a man who perseveres under trial; for once he has been approved, he will receive the crown of life which the Lord has promised to those who love Him* (verse 12).

A believer who perseveres in his walk with Jesus—even during the most grueling temptations and persecution—he is "blessed", i.e., he receives divine favor. Compare Job as a case in point: his case speaks volumes when it comes to this spiritual truth!

Job suffered more than most any of us ever will. He didn't lose only his wealth, but also his health. And it didn't end there. He also lost his children to death. As if to throw salt on the wound, Job's only remaining comforters either told him to curse God and die (his wife), or to admit that he caused all of his circumstances by doing wrong to all the folks around him (his three "friends", and a young man who accompanied them to "comfort" Job).

Oh me, oh my. The end of the day is nigh. (How's that for good poetry? lol) We must needs call it a day. But we will finish up this issue in our next study. Let's enjoy Jesus for a while now, before we fall asleep in His everlasting arms.

James 1:12-13

We were engaged in Job's predicament, when our last study drew to a close. Job lost all of his wealth, and all of his children too, and that in one fell swoop of disaster. Then his wife and friends all joined in chorus to sing,

> Job sinned, Job sinned;
> The no-good Job, he cannot win.
> Get to it, Job, curse God and die;
> And then when you're done, spit in His eye!

Even after he lost everything, including the folks closest to him, Job's struggles didn't break him. Job never once denounced God and turned to idols. But he did sin by questioning God's love for him. We know of no one who could do better in Job's dire straits than he did. So we won't pile any more of man's wisdom on Job.

But in terms of what really matters, God didn't condemn Job! He did correct Job about questioning God's wisdom, But then God restored Job into His fellowship. As for Job's three friends who judged Job's heart and condemned him, God demanded they first go to Job to confess their own sins against him. Then Job would pray for them and God would restore them (aka a guilt offering).

That is the sort of scenario Pastor James alludes to in verse 12 of today's text. Job was "blessed", you see. His grueling struggles did not define him: his relationship with God did. Because he really belonged to God, he persevered and received God's blessing all over again. Jump ahead to the last chapter in Job and see how much wealth, and how many children, Job wound up with. Job came out ahead!

The crown of life. What is that? First, what it is not. God doesn't save us provisionally; so long as we don't sin anymore, we stay saved. But woe is us should we prove to be true human beings, those conceived in sin and born in iniquity (cf., Psalm 51:5).

By that scenario the phrase *crown of life* sees "life" as that of eternity, and the *crown of life* as the reward of eternal life itself. The believer doesn't permanently receive the *crown of life* (eternal life itself), until his life on earth concludes and he is shown to have persevered through it all. That's not God's plan of salvation!

Scripture employs two Greek words which are translated "crown". One such word is διάδημα, written in English as *diadema*. Do you see our English word *diadem* there? This means our English word is a *transliteration*, not a *translation*.

A *translation* replaces the Greek word with an English word which means the same thing (e.g., διάδημα = "crown"). A *transliteration* keeps the Greek word and changes the Greek letters to English letters which sound the same (e.g., διάδημα becomes *diadem*).

The other Greek word translated "crown" is στέφανος. This is written in English as *stephanos*, from which comes our English names *Stephen, Stefan,* and *Stephanie* (transliterations).

The difference between these two Greek words is that a *diadem* is a crown worn by emperors and other political rulers. The Pope's headpiece is termed a *diadem*, which speaks volumes about the Roman Catholic view of one believer's authority over another.

The Greek *stephanos*, contrariwise, was used for the laurel wreaths which the victors in the Greek Olympic games received. Rather than a political ruler's symbol of authority (as per the *diadem*), the *stephanos* was a symbol of hard effort resulting in success.

Now guess which Greek word for "crown" is used in verse 12 of today's text. Go on. Give it a shot. Yes, ma'am, you on our right.

What's that you say? It's the Greek word *diadema*? Would you please name the church of which you are a member? You belong to St. Merric Catholic Church. Who would've guessed it? In the vein of the old *StarKist Tuna* commercials, "Sorry, Charlie, but you're not good enough to be a *StarKist* tuna." Wrong answer, ma'am.

By the process of elimination, we are left with the Greek word for "crown", *stephanos*, the laurel wreath which the winning athlete received after beating out the competition. Is the spiritual truth of this verse coming into focus for you yet? The issue in this case is not how the believer will rule with Jesus. No, but it is the believer as he is rewarded for running the race and winning the prize.

And no, the prize (i.e., the *stephanos* or "crown of life") is not eternal life. Every believer received that at the moment he was born again. He was baptized in the Holy Spirit as a body-part in the Church, the Body of Christ on earth during the Church Age. In this spiritual organism (the Church), each person is either the Head or another part of the Body. Hint: Jesus is the Head, we the Body.

This is invisible spiritual truth taught by means of visible physical realties. A head, and the body to which it is united, are used to represent King Jesus and the Church. The Church here is not a local congregation. The Church here is the universal Church, the invisible Church. This Church is not "invisible" as in no one can see her. Rather, she is "invisible" as in she is made up of every person who is truly born again.

Many folks in the local congregations sincerely think they are going to heaven, but they haven't been born again. No mere human being can see the heart of anyone; so none of us can make a determination as to who is, and who isn't, saved. Jesus presented this spiritual truth by His parable of the end times. He will come to the earth again, and send His angels to separate the wheat and the weeds. The wheat (the good fruit of the field) will be gathered into Jesus' silo, and the weeds will be cast into the fire to be burned up.

Jesus used parables to teach spiritual truths about the Church, as well as about His people who are not a part of the Church. They either lived before the Church Age, or they will live after it during the Tribulation Period and Millennium.

Someone just wondered, "What about those who are born after the Millennium, teacher?" In keeping with Rule #2 for Bible study we respond to you, sir, "What does your Bible tell you?" The answer is, "It doesn't." So we are not qualified to tell you either.

Still, there are strong indications in Scripture that, following the Millennium, a new heaven and new earth will be created, wherein sin does not dwell. Only those who have been born again, and who have received a new spiritual body (aka been glorified), will be allowed entrance into this new creation.

And we have it on good authority that heaven and earth, time and eternity, will become one by means of that event. Lastly, the angels don't procreate because they never die, so there is no more repopulation via new births. So will it be with everyone who gets to enjoy the new heaven and new earth through all eternity. This being the case, there will be no people born after the Millennium.

We address these issues in *Revelation: Volume 11* of our *Heavenly Citizens* series. Come join us in our class. All of our books are available at https://randyg555.wixsite.com/heavenly-citizens/shop. We look forward to your company as we study this Bible book.

One last note on *the crown of life.* We can still recall our earthly father's headstone in the cemetery. He was taken to heaven in 1959, so we strain our mental RAM to recall it. In addition to the standard information for headstones—you know, name, date of birth, and date of death—it had a quotation of these precious words from the *Book of Revelation,*

> *Be faithful until death, and I will give you the crown of life* [Revelation 2:10].

The crown of life ≠ eternal life. Everyone who is truly born again already has that. We received it at the moment we were born again. And as we just learned, only true believers (the wheat) will gain entrance into heaven. Those who are religious, who believe they are God's people but are not (the weeds), will be cast into the fire.

That is what the crown of life is not. The crown of life = a victory garland given to those who spiritually mature as disciples of King Jesus. They spend time with Him regularly, getting to know who He is as a Person and learning His will for their life personally. They do this because they love Him and want to cease being the old sinner who lives for self, and increasingly grow into the new creation who lives for Jesus.

The victory wreath known as the crown of life will go to those who have such a heart for King Jesus. It is the believer's reward for service to our King. In the **context** of the *Book of James,* the phrase *crown of life* is given to the believer who goes through the persecution which the world inflicts on believers because they are believers. Those who don't apostatize, but who instead persevere, receive this victory wreath.

One last detail is in order here. The crown of life is promised by King Jesus *to those who love Him.* Does that not portray the true believer as we depicted him two paragraphs prior?

In Revelation 2:4 the believers of Ephesus *lost their first love.* They stopped having their personal relationship with Jesus (see the behavior depicted three paragraphs prior). Oh, but they still did all of their good works "for Jesus", and even more good works too! This is followed by a depiction of the believers in Smyrna, who signify "the persecuted Church" (cf., Revelation 2:8-11). These are the believers who were exhorted,

> *Be faithful until death, and I will give you <u>the crown of life</u>* [Revelation 2:10].

Do you see the flow of thought there? Waddaya mean no? It's there! The first step in a believer backsliding is to be so active as he "serves Jesus", that he hasn't time to actually be alone with Jesus where he maintains his first love for Jesus. Consequently, he becomes ritualistic and formal, merely religious though so sincere.

In order to spiritually resuscitate this believer, King Jesus responds with CPR ("Christ Power Revival"). He grants permission to the wicked one to persecute the lukewarm believer, so that he might be shocked out of his spiritual doldrums and restored into right relationship with the King. Hence the identifier "the persecuted Church". Those who respond with confession and repentance are restored. They are the believers who receive the crown of life.

Note well the significance of the last clause in verse 12? It reads,

> *...the crown of life which the Lord has promised to those who love Him* (verse 12).

What's that you say? You don't see any significance. It's like this. In the phrase "the crown of life", both nouns (crown, life) are singular in the Greek. In the phrase "those who love Him", the Greek is plural to identify true believers ("those who love"), while the recipient of their love (Him) is singular to identify King Jesus.

What does this mean? It means there is only one "crown of life", but there are numerous, even countless multitudes of believers, those who love their King. How can multitudes of believers wear one crown of life? Answer: they can't. Then the crown of life cannot be eternal life itself, or only one person can be truly saved in the end! (I hope it's me!)

The crown of life is not eternal life, which every believer shares by virtue of being "in Christ". The crown of life is the believer's reward for serving Jesus. The phrase is symbolic. It represents the Lord's approval on the believer, based on his service to the King.

While still on the earth, he lived the eternal life which lives in Him since rebirth, by serving Jesus as portrayed earlier in this study. King Jesus rewards him by giving him a new ministry in eternity to continue serving Him. How well (or not) each true believer served the King in time and space, that will be the measuring rod for how much authority, how impactful the ministry, he will receive from the King in eternity, as he serves Him there.

Our hearts are stirred by the description of true believers at the *Bema*, as seen by King Jesus in eternity. We are said to be *those who love Him* (verse 12). The Greek verb translated "love" there is *agapao*. The noun form of it is *agape*. Perhaps you are familiar with this Greek noun. It refers to God's love, in contrast to man's form of "love" (*philia* in the Greek).

God's love is clearly delineated from man's in John 3:16, *For God so loved the world, that He gave…* Sinful man doesn't desire to have a mate so that he can love her (or her him). No! Sinful man wants someone so <u>he</u> won't be lonely, so <u>he</u> can have help in life, so <u>he</u>… And the list could be extended ad infinitum.

God already has all there is. Everything belongs to Him. He does not need to get anything from us mere mortals. God's love GIVES; it doesn't TAKE. All have sinned, all have gone astray, even we believers. Self still lurks inside us believers, so we still TAKE.

This is why we have to spiritually mature into the image of Jesus and be transformed by the renewing of the mind. God's love in us, His *agape*, must grow, so that we too GIVE to others, rather than continue to TAKE from them.

The old sinner inside the believer = the weeds; the new creation of Christ in the believer, the hope of glory = the wheat. Only by time alone with Jesus can the believer cultivate the field of his new life, so that the weeds don't choke the wheat, leaving him spiritually unfruitful. To cultivate the field of your new life, you must,

> *Establish a spiritual regimen of daily quiet time alone with Jesus, Bible open and man's books closed, with hands folded in prayer.*

Now let us press on and enter the next field of our labors.

> *Let no one say when he is tempted, "I am being tempted by God"; for God cannot be tempted by evil, and He Himself does not tempt anyone* (verse 13).

Let us begin with the beginning, a sensible approach, we do say. The beginning of any passage, Bible or otherwise, is to be had from Rule #1 for Bible study, which teaches,

> *A text without a context is a pretext.*

What, then, is the **context** for verse 13 of today's text? As the famous secret agent Maxwell Smart was wont to phrase the matter, "Would you believe…?" Yes, would you believe the context for verse 13 is verses 2-12? Well, it is!

A believer facing temptation is being tested by God. This allows him to spiritually mature, by learning to rely on God, instead of on self, for victory. In eternity he will be rewarded accordingly.

Isn't it remarkable, at how young an age every person learns how to rationalize his sins, shuffle the feet and make excuses and blame the person next to him. We've all heard it, haven't we, parents?

> *Timmy, who hit the baseball through the neighbor's window? Speak up, boy!*

> *I cannot tell a lie, pa. Joey threw me a bad pitch. It's his fault!*

Been there, done that. From our text it is apparent that the same rationalizations we have today prevailed back in the day. The Holy Spirit instructs the believer,

> *You'll be blessed at the Bema by the reward Jesus gives you for your service to Him. But you must persevere in putting the flesh under heel, so that you overcome the testing of your faith which Jesus allows in your life.*

Without hesitation the believer counters,

> *Joey threw me a bad pitch. It's his fault. (read, "God made me do it. If He didn't bring those pesky temptations into my life, I wouldn't sin!")*

That is the sense of the caveat,

> *Let no one say when he is tempted, "I am being tempted by God"* (verse 13)

In plain-speak that reads, "It's God's fault. He tempted me!" The Greek word three times translated as "tempted" is a form of the verb *peirazo*. In verse 2 it was the noun *peirasmos*, translated "trials". Here it is translated "tempted". This verifies what we learned earlier in these studies, that "trials", "temptations", and "tests" are all the same Greek word in the New Testament.

This is significant how? Just this. On many occasions we have encountered believers who insist that God tests us, but (they then assert) He never (as in not ever) tempts us. The difference, by their telling of it, is that a test is a good thing, while a temptation is a bad thing.

Don't you find man's words about the Bible to be so plain black and white, brothers and sisters? If the same Greek word is used in translating all three of those English words—and the text was originally inspire by the Holy Spirit in Greek—then how is it that one time it means a good thing and another a bad thing?

We'll tell you what the answer is <u>not</u>. It's not because the Greek language defines it as good one time and bad another time. It's because we translate it as if it infers a good thing one time and a bad thing another time.

The point for us to realize is that the Bible does <u>not</u> teach that God never tempts anyone. But we cannot explain why and why not in today's lesson because today is over! Let us betake ourselves to the feet of Jesus for a while, before having a refreshing time of sleep in His presence. We will meet back here tomorrow to continue this discussion, same time, same station.

James 1:13-15

Our last study concluded in the middle of the stream. Again! We just must stop doing that. The saddle sores are too much at our advanced age. We squirmed the entire night, as if we had a bad case of hemorrhoids! So let's get to riding, so we can be done and mercifully climb off this saddle.

Our colloquy has been about how the Bible doesn't teach that God never tempts anyone. If we shrewdly replace a proper translation ("tempt") with a euphemism ("test" or "try"), people conclude that the Bible does teach it. By that reckoning, God only does nice things, like "test" or "try" us. But "tempt" us like some big old meanie? Never! Interpretation, not translation, does that.

We don't mean to say that the meaning given by our translations is wrong, that these translations teach what the Bible doesn't. We are saying that Bible translation isn't supposed to interpret the text: it is supposed to put the text into English as nearly literal as possible, while still being readable to the English reader.

> *Heretic! That's what you are, teacher! It says right there in verse 12 that God doesn't tempt anyone. So begone with your evil self!*

We have been met with words to that effect, when we teach this basic Bible reality. Yes, it's true. Verse 13 reads that God never tempts anyone…until it doesn't. Or as the proverb phrases it,

> *The first to plead his case seems right, until another comes and examines him* [Proverbs 18:17].

We've spent considerable paper and ink (or computer bytes) in this lesson and yesterday's, to show how the Greek word translated "tempt" also means "test" or "try". It's a matter of the translator deciding which definition to use. He does so based on the **context** in which the Greek word is used. Ergo, he uses the English word "tempt" when he decides a bad thing is occurring. When he sees good things are involved, he switches to the words "test" or "try".

But the Holy Spirit didn't use different words throughout the New Testament, to distinguish good things from bad. As translator, man did. As English readers of the New Testament, our job is to make a decision about whether or not the translators chose correctly. Is the context indeed a "good" thing, or is it a "bad" thing?

Alas, but oftentimes believers don't rightly divide the Word of Truth; so they see something as "bad" when it is "good". Or they miss the mark and fail to see that its condition is decided not by the thing in itself, but by man's response to it. For example, is the Gospel a good or a bad thing?

> *Teacher, now we know you are a Samaritan and have a demon inside you! The Gospel is a good thing. Period! Never is it a bad thing, you false prophet, you!*

Ouch. Now our feelings are hurt. But not to be detoured from the path of light, we resort to Rule #2 for Bible study which teaches,

> *The Bible is our sole and final authority in all matters of faith and practice.*

This means that our opinion isn't the authority on truth. The Word of God is. So, then, what does God say about the goodness (or not) of the Gospel? Let's hear the Holy Spirit tell it in His own words:

> *For we are a fragrance of Christ to God among those who are being saved and among those who are perishing; to the one an aroma from death to death, to the other an aroma from life to life* [2 Corinthians 2:15-16].

Try and tell unbelievers, who wind up in hell, that the Gospel is a "good" thing! The same Gospel seed is sown in the unbeliever as is sown in the believer. To one it becomes *an aroma from life to life,* to the other *an aroma from death to death.* To one eternal life with God in heaven is the result; to the other it's eternal death, separated from God in the lake of fire. For one the Gospel is a "good" thing, you see, for the other a "bad" thing.

How is this so? The answer is to be had in the phrases *from life to life* and *from death to death,* with the operative words being the prepositions "from" and "to". The fragrance of the Gospel is "from" Christ" and "to" sinful man.

For those who hear the Gospel and receive Christ as their sin offering, they have risen out of the empty tomb as new creations "in Christ". Consequently, in the case of believers, eternal <u>life</u> came "from" Christ "to" them, resulting in them also having <u>life</u>.

For those who hear the Gospel and reject Christ as their sin offering, Christ's death has no "good" benefit for them. His death on the cross for sins comes "from" Him "to" them. By rejecting it as payment for the penalty of their sins, they remain in their sins. Consequently, they continue to be dead in trespasses and sins, the state in which they were physically born. Christ's life never comes to them, you see. Only His death does as judgment on their sins.

This is how one situation is a "good" thing to some, and at the same time a "bad" thing to others. It requires interpretation on our part to make a proper choice. But the English words "tempt", "try", and "test" are not in the Greek (or in three different Greek words). So this understanding that God never "tempts" anyone isn't based on a right understanding of Scripture. It grows out of man's words.

Now let's take our vetting of this issue even deeper. Let's consider verse 13 of today's text and cull the spiritual truth it affords us.

If we interpret the text as Occidentals, by inviting Aristotle to the party to explain it to us, we will latch onto the distinctions between the English words "test", "try", and "tempt". It seems to solve the matter for us, so why not?

Why not? Why not? How about because Pastor James was not an Occidental but a Biblical Jew, and Biblical Jews were dyed-in-the-wool Orientals. They didn't much care for Aristotle, thank you very much. Aristotle never received an invite from them to Sabbath lunch, where everyone sat around the dinner table conversing about the Word of God.

By Oriental reckoning, there is no confusion in verse 13. Just keep in mind that the **context** for the verse is the Oriental mode of reasoning, and all confusion dissipates like the dew on the grass on a hot summer morn. Occidentals think in terms of chronology. Orientals tend to place similar concepts together, and who cares if one occurred right after another or several years later!

Let's apply this to verse 13 now. We will diagram it so we can better visualize it:

> A. Let no one say when he is tempted,
> B. "I am being tempted by God";
> A. for God cannot be tempted by evil,
> B. and He Himself does not tempt anyone

Ah, yes. Once we diagram the sentences, we discover that it takes the form of Biblical Hebrew poetry. Today we rhyme words at the end of lines as our form of poetry. In the Bible the Hebrews rhyme ideas within lines as their form of poetry.

The rhymed ideas are seen as running "parallel" to each other. For similar ideas the name *synonymous parallelism* applies. If the ideas are dissimilar, the title *antonymous parallelism* is attached.

Focus on the two "A"s and the two "B"s which precede those four lines in our diagram above. The concept of "parallelism" is that the ideas somehow correlate with one another. This means the two "A" lines correlate with one another in some way, as do the two "B" lines. How do they correlate in our diagram above?

First the two "A" lines. A believer is undergoing temptation in his life (the first "A" line). Unlike the believer, God cannot be tempted (the second "A" line). Implied = let the believer rely on the new life of God in him, in order to be victorious over the temptation.

Now the two "B" lines. During his temptation, let not the believer accuse God of being the cause of his temptation (the first "B" line). God doesn't tempt anyone with evil (the second "B" line). It stands to reason that, since God doesn't tempt anyone with evil, He isn't the source of the believer's evil temptation.

The distinction in the two "B" lines is this: the believer is the one who is tempted by evil in the first "B" line; in the second "B" line God is seen as the One who can't tempt anyone with evil. Implied = God is always on His throne, but man is still free to choose.

The distinction between the "A" lines is <u>the issue of being tempted</u>. Remember, the **context** for verse 13 is verse 12, in which the believer "perseveres" under "trial" (aka temptation). Verse 13 follows this with a believer who "fails" when he is tempted (i.e., he doesn't persevere). His reaction is to blame God for it!

In the first "A" line the believer is tempted and fails. In the second "A" line God never tempts with evil. It is not in His DNA. Temptation to commit evil cannot interest Him, so He is incapable of passing the evil onto others.

In summation, verse 13 occurs in the context of verse 12. Two parties are contrasted with each other, and two opposite results occur. One party is "God", the accused instigator of the results. The other party is a believer who fails when inveigled.

Do you see what this analysis reveals about the concept of God never tempting anyone? No, no, no. We won't allow a perplexed face here. Focus on the four lines of our diagram above. Muse on it. Is the issue that of "temptation" as an abstraction? No, it is not!

The issue in verse 13 is "tempting with evil". Hence the reason why the translators chose the English word "tempt" to translate the Greek verb *peirazo* (verse 13), but chose to translate the Greek noun *peirasmos* as "trial" rather than as "temptation" (verse 12).

If we include the implication in our translation—an implication which is obvious by Oriental reckoning—verse 13 reads thusly:

> *...for God cannot be tempted by evil, and He Himself does not tempt anyone <u>with evil</u>* (verse 13[b]).

We added the underlined words. They are implied by the context, which is standard fare in Oriental reasoning. So yes, God does too "tempt" folks, but His form of temptation is never "evil". It is always righteous. It is up to the one "tempted" to respond in an appropriate manner to the temptation.

God's intentions are that the believer respond by seeking God's deliverance from the temptation, which spiritually matures him. That is a "good" thing. If the believer responds by focusing on the temptation instead of on God, then he fails the spiritual test. This strengthens the old sinner still inside the believer, so that he lives carnally (i.e., walks in the flesh). That is a "bad" thing.

All of these "temptations" (aka "trials" or "tests") are a part of God rearing His kids to spiritual maturity. We are what we choose. It is up to each one of us to choose King Jesus over self. That's the test.

The New Testament employs two Greek words translated "evil":

- *kakos* (the root and vine of evil)
- *poneros* (the fruit of evil)

In verse 13 God is said to be immune to *kakos*, from the evil itself. Think of it like this. Man is born with "sin", and so he "sins". The "sin" with which he is born = a "sin nature", which is the root and vine of sinful acts. When he commits an individual "sin", it is the fruit of his "sin nature". So man doesn't commit a "sin" and so become a "sinner". He is born a "sinner", and sinners sin; they don't live righteously.

In God's case it is the opposite. God is not a sinner, so he never (as in not ever) sins. God is righteous, so He only thinks, says, and does right. He <u>is</u> (i.e., His Person), so He <u>does</u> (i.e., His Ministry). Pastor James phrases it as God being *apeirastos* (verse 13), "not able to be tempted" by evil in its very nature (evil, the root and vine). If the essence of evil (its root and vine) cannot get to God, its fruit (individual cases of evil) are even less able to do so.

Consider the import of this spiritual truth. Some of us are tempted by sexual lust, but not by alcohol and drugs. This doesn't make us only a "partial sinner", whatever that is! When we have the infectious disease known as "sin", the infection taints us all over.

Verse 14 forcibly states that God cannot be tempted by sin at its root. If the other Greek word for "evil" had been used here, it would amount to saying that God cannot be tempted by some sins, or by individual acts of sin, calling into question God's immunity from sin in its essence. The Greek word *kakos* (the root and vine of evil) is required in order to rightly portray God's Person.

> *But each one is tempted when he is carried away and enticed by his own lust* [verse 14].

The flow of the text is straightforward enough. Its meaning serves to confirm that we are on the right track by our analysis of the prior verses. A believer falls for a temptation. He responds by blaming God for tempting him. After all, God is in charge. God is testing his faith. God set him up to fail by giving him more than he could bear. His failure to persevere proves it!

Not so, O believer. Not so. God is incapable of being tempted by evil. No one can give to another what he doesn't first have for himself. God cannot be tempted by evil, so he cannot give such a temptation (i.e., "to do evil") to anyone else.

Whence, then, cometh the temptation in the believer to do evil? Ah, and a right fine question it is too. This is where verses 14 and 15 come into play here. These two verses answer that question, which is why verses 14-15 follow verses 12-13. Since verse 15 attaches to verse 14 so snugly, let's read it at this time and interpret them as one unit.

> *Then when lust has conceived, it gives birth to sin; and when sin is accomplished, it brings forth death* (verse 15).

God didn't tempt you with evil, O believer. The temptation found a successful entrance into your life through the door of "your own lust" (verse 14). Busted! Exposed for the sinners we are, all we believers.

The *Doctrine of Christian Perfectionism* is manmade hogwash. Don't fall for it. When it approaches from one direction, mimic Joseph when Potiphar's wife plied him with explicit sexual desires. Run! Flee as fast as you can in the other direction! Get out of there as if you very life depends on it because it does!

No believer ever becomes totally without sin this side of eternity. Christians become "perfected" at the Rapture. This is the event when King Jesus comes in the clouds and calls all believers to come to Him in the clouds, so He can take us home to heaven to meet His Father. That is what a gentleman does, when he decides to marry, you know. He introduces his fiancée to his parents.

Anyway, at the moment the believers begin to rise from the earth to go to Jesus in the clouds, their natural bodies of sin instantly metamorphose into their righteous spiritual bodies of eternity. Jesus has been clothed in His spiritual body since His resurrection. It is the same kind of spiritual body we will have too at the Rapture. But until then, believers still wear the old body of sin, with all of its susceptibility to sin. Ergo, we are capable of being *enticed by our own lust* (verse 14).

The Greek verb translated "carried away" takes us back to days of idyllic childhood. We would snatch earthworms as they crawled out of the ground, following a summer rain. Then we gathered our fishing poles and hied off to the creek to get us some catfish.

Well, guess what? The fish didn't jump onto our fishhook, just because we desired to catch them. We had to attach an earthworm to the hook and dangle it before their eyes, as they swam in the creek. A shiny hook and sinker helped by glittering in the water to get their attention.

This is the sense of the Greek verb translated "carried away". Our "own lust" is the catfish. The temptation is the shiny hook with the worm attached. Our catfish, er, we mean "our own lust", is "carried away" by that earthworm dangling before our eyes. The animal nature of man (i.e., the dust of the ground) is no better than a catfish, you see. It automatically responds to its fleshly cravings.

The Greek verb translated "carried away" denotes the fish's natural impulse drawing it to the worm. The Greek verb for "enticed" suggests the end result for the catfish: it is caught on the hook.

Not a pretty picture of us believers, is it? We are not exactly flattered to be portrayed as no better than a catfish. A catfish? Really? But yes, a catfish…or any mere brute beast, brothers and sisters.

Still, there is a saving grace to this condition for believers. Unlike the old life, we are now born again. The old sinner cannot help but sin because all he has is a sin nature. The new believer received the new nature of the Holy Spirit in him, at the time he was born again.

So yes, he still has the ability to sin ("his own lust"); but he also has the Holy Spirit living in him, who only loves righteousness and is all-powerful. Ergo, He can give the believer victory over the old sinner. However, there is this caveat. God never forces any person to be saved, and He never forces any believer to live as saved. When temptation appeals to "his own lust", the believer has to choose whom he will serve: his own lust or King Jesus.

The difference is that there is no choice for the unbeliever to make: he is not capable of living righteously! The believer, contrariwise, is enabled by Holy Spirit power to live righteously, while he is also tempted by his sin nature to commit sins. But not to fret, O believer! The day is coming, and is right at the door, when the voice like a trumpet will sound from the mouth of King Jesus, *Come up here!* We will be divested of our body of sin and clothed in our spiritual body; and never again will that old traitor, the sin nature in us, tempt us to sin.

Oh, dear, our time is up for today. The remainder of the process by which believers stumble into sin (verse 15) must needs wait for the next study. But the good thing is that we can now spend time alone with Jesus and His Word. So let's take advantage of the invite.

James 1:15-16

Believers are like catfish. Not a flattering self-image, is it? The good news is twofold. First, no longer do we have to be so. Secondly, a time is soon coming when we will never again be so. Hallelujah! Praise the Lord! Even so, come quickly, Lord Jesus.

Verse 12 warns the believer that, in the world, he will have trials, temptations, struggles in life, and he needs to persevere through them to victory. Verse 13 then adds, "But don't go to blaming God when you don't persevere!"

Consider the remarkable resemblance between verses 12-13 of today's text, and 1 John 2:1-2. The Apostle John writes, *I write these things to you so that you don't sin. But if anyone sins…*

See! That's the same thing as Pastor James teaches in verses 12-13 of today's text. He says, "The believer is to persevere over sin in his life. But when he doesn't…"

In both cases the believer is expected not to sin. Nonetheless, every believer will fail on occasion, so the Holy Spirit tells the believer what to do about it when he does sin. We learn from this that no believer ever fully attains to perfection this side of eternity. This doesn't excuse our sins or make light of them. It addresses the spiritual reality of the believer still living in a sinful world in a body of sin, and gives him directions back to his Savior for forgiveness and restoration when he sins.

Following this teaching (verses 12-13), Brother James then spells out in no uncertain terms the process by which a believer sins. It begins with an earthworm, a fishhook, and a catfish, er, we mean with a temptation and the believer's "own lust". Whence cometh this lust? Answer: from the body of sin in which he still resides.

That is how far we went in our last study. We will now continue from where we left off yesterday.

Then when lust has conceived, it gives birth to sin; and when sin is accomplished, it brings forth death (verse 15).

Let's employ a numbered list to keep track of the progression of sin, as it advances in a human being.

1. the temptation
2. his own lust is attracted by it
3. his own lust is hooked on it
4. his own lust is impregnated with it
5. his own lust births sin

That is the progression of sin in a person's life, as per verses 14-15. What a smack-down of the impenitent believer who sins, and then thinks to blame God for it! You go, Pastor James. You're the man! Or rather, the Holy Spirit is the man. He inspired it.

All of us parents can relate. Imagine the child. Ma and pa pour their lives into him, teaching him to be born again, and to spend time with the Lord Jesus so as to know Him increasingly better.

Then one day their son does wrong. Oh, he had done wrong often enough before; but this time is different. When confronted about his wrongdoing, he doesn't even offer a whimper in pretense of being sorry. No, but he looks dad and mom in the eye and says,

It's your fault, ma and pa. You made me do it! You should have given me what I wanted,; then I wouldn't have had to take it against your express instructions.

Been there, done that. So have my kids. You know your kids have also done so, parents. It's called human nature (or the sin nature for short). It exists in every person born of Adam the First—which includes the entire human race, Jesus excepted. God is Jesus' Father, as the Holy Spirit miraculously created sinless human semen in the Jewish virgin Miriam.

Yes, we parents should expect our kids to sin at times. We are not being real if we don't! That isn't what hurts the most. It is the sin of defiance which goes deep down into the soul, breaking the heart of us parents. It is the equivalent of a person having a fatal disease, and he refuses the cure because he denies having any disease, even though it is visible to everyone who sees him.

Does this help you to enter into the heart of God, brothers and sisters? We are guilty! As the prophet Nathan told King David, when he committed adultery with Bathsheba and had her husband Uriah murdered because of it, "You are the man! You committed those grievous acts!" (cf., 2 Samuel 12)

Messiah Jesus spoke a parable to illustrate this condition of all humankind. All of us know it as *The Prodigal Son*. But this title misses the main point.

There was this wealthy father, and he had two sons. One took his inheritance and went off faraway, where he could live in ways which disrespected his father and besmirched his good name.

The other son stayed at home with his father, doing his chores like a good ol' boy was expected to do. He learned the ropes well and followed the expected routine to a T.

One day the runaway (or prodigal) son came to his senses and returned home. His motives weren't pure: he squandered his inheritance and had to feed pigs in order to feed himself. His predicament conjured memories of dad and home and food to eat. Even dad's servants had plenty of food! So back home he went.

Even more though, he truly realized how bad a boy he had been to his dad. He wasn't fit to be dad's son any longer. So when his dad saw him coming down the road back to home, and ran down the road to meet him and give him a big hug, the prodigal son begged only that he could be one of dad's servants.

Balderdash! Dad would have none of it. No, dad didn't send the kid packing. He refused to make him a servant. He was a son, dad's son, and he always would be.

That much is taught in nearly every sermon and Sunday School lesson about this story. But even though it takes up the majority of the tale, it isn't the main point. To get the main point, we must needs resort to Rule #1 for Bible study, which teaches,

> *A text without a context is a pretext.*

What, then, is the **context** for *The Prodigal Son*. We needn't guess or quibble over the answer, brothers and sisters. The Holy Spirit spelled it out for us in plain-speak. Listen to how this story began.

> *Now all the tax collectors and the sinners were coming near Him to listen to Him. Both the Pharisees and the scribes began to grumble, saying, "This man receives sinners and eats with them." So He told them this parable* [Luke 15:1-3].

Jesus' story had three main characters in the cast. There was the father, and a runaway son, and a stay-at-home son. (Today we would say he lived in mom's basement!)

The context for it, as per Luke 15 above, also lists three main characters. There was Jesus teaching the Word of God. There were also the tax collectors and sinners listening to Jesus teach the Word of God. Lastly, there were the Pharisees and the scribes.

Here's the thing about the Pharisees and the scribes. They didn't come to hear Jesus teach the Word of God. They came to find fault with Jesus, even when there was no fault to be found. They adhered to the old adage, "Never waste a good crisis!"

So the Pharisees and the scribes came to the event, and first created a crisis, then fanned the flames to discredit Jesus and turn folks against Him. That was their goal for all things, as they pertained to Jesus. Consider anything and everything they said or did: getting rid of Jesus was the goal for it.

Well, the father in Jesus' story is Father God. He has two sons, or rather two groups of mankind who are represented by the two sons. On one hand are those who sin against God by disobeying His Word, and they know they do so. These folks equate to the tax collectors and sinners in the nation of Israel of Jesus' day, God's people under *Torah* (aka the Law of Moses).

On the other hand are those who sin against God, but hang out in the temple and synagogue. These dudes think this makes them right with Father God because they ritualistically go through the motions of "obeying *Torah*".

Truth be told, they interpreted God's Word as they saw fit, then obeyed to some extent what they said God wanted, and thought Father God must be pleased with them. To make matters even worse, they looked down the nose at the less fortunate Jews in their day, for not hanging out in the temple and synagogue! Needless to say, but these dudes equate with the Pharisees and the scribes.

The moral to the story is twofold, but the main point of the two is not the tax collectors and sinners coming to Jesus to hear Him teach the Word of God. Rather, it's the religious leaders and other folks who hang around in the church building and think this pleases God and makes them better than other folks.

The connection this has to verses 12-15 of James 1 is this. We noted how our kids become defiant at times when they do wrong, rather than even pretend to be sorry. They blame their parents for their wrongdoing, as if the parents forced them to do wrong.

In Biblical parlance this concept is known as *Mr. Impenitent*. In Jesus' parable of the prodigal son, the prodigal was the penitent, the older son the impenitent. When the prodigal returned to the father, dad gave him a feast and celebrated. His son had been lost; but no more! Now his son was found.

When the older son saw this feast given to his young brother, he resented dad for it even more than he resented his younger brother. Instead of being ecstatic that his younger brother returned home, and with a right heart too, older bro wished he stayed lost so he, the older brother, could be the center of attention in dad's life.

Why, older bro even looked more pious and respectful because of younger bro's ugly escapades. This stoked older bro's pride, as he fancied himself the darling-dear of dear old dad. But his no-good brother ruined it by worming his way back into dad's good graces, turning dad's attention from older bro. Who wouldn't resent that?

As Jesus explained it via the father's colloquy with his oldest son, the tax collectors and sinners wouldn't resent it. Their experience of being runaways from God resulted not only in them returning to Father God and being accepted back by Him; it also resulted in them experiencing the love of God, so that they had that same love of God for other runaways.

Those who would resent it were the Pharisees and the scribes, the Jewish religious authorities and other bigwigs of society, who received perks for being God's darlings. This arrangement came at the expense of everyone else in society; but so long as the perks stayed intact for the elites, who cared. Certainly not the elites!

God showed what His position is on the matter, when Son God (Jesus) told this tale in the **context** of the scenario which Brother Luke portrayed. Staying at home (read: hanging out in the church building), and fitting into a ritualistic role of dos and don'ts, does not please Father God. He created us in His image so we could relate to Him and become like Him. God doesn't hang out in the church building and behave according to a set of rules!

James was a Jew steeped in Jewish life. His mores were founded on *Torah* (aka the Law of Moses). He wrote this letter to Jewish believers who lived in the *diaspora* (the Gentile lands). It was standard fare for the Jews of Gospel times, to think of the Gentiles in the same way the scribes and Pharisees thought of the tax collectors and sinners.

Pastor James knows the feeling only too well. Consequently, he wants the Jewish believers in Gentile lands to be aware of it, and work on their attitude problem with the Gentiles who live around them. Fixing that attitude problem was preliminary to sharing Jesus with them. He also wants them to be aware of it so they don't blame God for their sin of hating the Gentiles who persecute them.

Before venturing forth in the text, a synopsis of our numbered list above is in order. We will begin with repeating the list for the sake of memory:

1. the temptation
2. his own lust is attracted by the temptation
3. his own lust is hooked on the temptation
4. his own lust is impregnated with the temptation
5. his own lust births sin

That is the progression of sin in a person's life, for both believers and unbelievers. It begins with Point #1, and proceeds point by point to Point #5, where sin is born. Let's explain each point:

Point #1: the temptation. Sinful man is tempted *by his own lust* (verse 14). Lust = any inordinate desire for something. The noun *inordinate* means that it is excessive or immoderate, uncontrolled or unrestrained. In other words the sinner surrenders control and allows the temptation to have its way in his life.

Sin began in the garden in the east at the dawn of human history. Consequently, we should see <u>lust</u> <u>in</u> <u>action</u> in the account of that first sin. And we do! It consists of three areas of human existence, and all three are stated quite lucidly in Genesis 3:6. The Apostle John reiterates them just as lucidly in 1 John 2:16.

In order to be the Savior of sinners, Messiah Jesus (<u>the</u> <u>last</u> <u>Adam</u>; cf., 1 Corinthians 15:45) endured the same temptations <u>the</u> <u>first</u> <u>Adam</u> did, via his wife Eve and his siding with her over the Lord God (cf., Matthew 4:1-11). Unlike the first Adam, however, the last Adam, Messiah Jesus, rejected the temptations with which He was plied by the snake in the grass, Satan.

This issue is of the utmost importance, brothers and sisters. The writer to the Hebrews thought so (or rather the Holy Spirit did, so He inspired him to write that Bible book (cf., Hebrews 4:15).

Point #2: his own lust is attracted by the temptation. In the case of the first sin, this step in the progression of sin is depicted thusly, *When the woman saw* (cf., Genesis 3:6).

Point #3: his own lust is hooked on the temptation. In the case of the first sin, this step in the progression of sin is portrayed by these words, *the tree was good for food...a delight to the eyes...desirable to make one wise.*

Point #4: his own lust is impregnated with the temptation. In the case of the first sin, this step in the progression of sin is visualized in this fashion, *she took from its fruit.*

Point #5: his own lust births sin. In the case of the first sin, this last step in the progression of sin is consummated by the actual act of sinning (i.e., by disobeying God's Word), which is recorded simply as *and she ate*. God unequivocally instructed the man,

> *From any tree of the garden you may eat freely; but from the tree of the knowledge of good and evil <u>you</u> <u>shall</u> <u>not</u> <u>eat</u>, for in the day that you eat from it you will surely die* [Genesis 2:16-17].

The first Adam ate fruit from the **kogae tree** anyway (cf., Genesis 3:6). That was the actual first sin, the one which turned the first Adam into a sinner, which in turn made his offspring (all mankind) to be born sinners.

Don't overlook this important detail in our explication of the progression of sin. As we noted in our analysis of Point #1 (the temptation), Messiah Jesus also was tempted by the same three aspects of sin which the first Adam faced. As we also noted, the writer to the Hebrews emphasizes to us that Messiah Jesus was <u>tempted</u> in all points, just as we are, and yet He had no sin.

The spiritual truth to garner from this is that "temptation" itself <u>is</u> <u>not sin</u>. Sin does not take place until the actual act of disobeying God's Word. Hence the first sin was Point #5 of our list: *she ate*.

Now let us march onward in our text for today:

> *Do not be deceived, my beloved brethren. Every good thing given and every perfect gift is from above, coming down from the Father of lights, with whom there is no variation or shifting shadow* (verses 16-17).

My beloved brethren. The Greek noun translated "brethren" is *adelphos*. The New Testament uses it spiritually as a synonym for

"Christian" or "a believer". Occasionally it refers to natural-birth siblings, but almost always to spiritual-rebirth siblings.

Not only are the recipients of this letter believers, but they are "beloved". The Greek word is *agapetos*, an adjectival form of the noun *agape*, which is employed in the New Testament to identify the "love" of God vs. the "love" (*philia*) of man. God's love <u>gives</u> to others (cf., John 3:16). Man's love <u>takes</u> from others.

God is "love" (or *agape*; cf., 1 John 4:8). As like begets like in God's economy, each thing produces after its own kind. Ergo, since God is love (*agape*), whoever is born again of God is also love (the noun *agape*). We believers are siblings in the Family of God. We are "beloved" (the adjective *agapetos*). We are to spiritually mature to where our lifestyle consists of "giving" ourselves to each other, which is the definition of *agape*, not habitually "taking" from each other. What say we grow into the image of Jesus in this manner.

Do not be deceived (verse 16). The Greek verb is a present tense imperative. This makes it both a command and one which is to be obeyed continuously throughout the believer's life. We could paraphrase it like this: *Be sure you reject any temptation in your life every single day!*

The flow of thought <u>from</u> verses 12-15 <u>to</u> verses 16-17 is about as consistent as consistent can be! But we will have to wait until our next study to see how this is so. We are out of time today, so we must draw this study to a close.

Be sure to <u>give</u> some time to King Jesus now. He misses you and wants to enjoy your company, even as He wants to <u>give</u> you His time so that you can enjoy Him too.

James 1:16-18

Our last study found us in the unenviable position of being in the middle of the stream again, sitting on a saddle atop our horse. Ouch! Those saddle sores are the worst! So without further delay, let's get right to it and extract ourselves from this precarious situation. We will begin by rereading the relevant portion of our text for today.

> *Do not be deceived, my beloved brethren. Every good thing given and every perfect gift is from above, coming down from the Father of lights, with whom there is no variation or shifting shadow* (verses 16-17).

We had just noted how the verb which begins verse 16 is a command to be obeyed continuously throughout our lifetime. The believer must guard himself, so that he never (as in not ever) succumbs to temptation and sins.

Then we noted how the flow of thought from verses 12-15 to verses 16-17 is about as smooth a segue as one could create. And that is where we stopped and spent the night on our saddle in the midst of the stream.

So how do verses 16-17 connect so smoothly to verses 12-15? Ah, and a right fine question it is too… A thousand pardons, please. We didn't know you were looking to us for the answer. We will be pleased to provide it to you. Sorry again for the delay.

The flow of thought in verses 12-15 goes like so. Every believer is tempted every day all day. After all, every believer does live in a body of sin in a world of sin. What else should we expect?

The unbeliever can only succumb to temptation. That is his nature (or his sin nature). The believer, too, still lives in a body of sin (i.e., the old sinner), and he will continue to do so until the Rapture, when his body of sin is instantaneously metamorphosed into his eternal spiritual body of physical resurrection.

The difference between the believer and unbeliever isn't that one has a body of sin and the other has a spiritual body…not while the believer walks this earth anyway! The difference is to be found in the new life which the believer received at rebirth.

The believer is baptized in the Holy Spirit, who evermore lives inside every believer. The Holy Spirit feeds the believer spiritual truth from the Bible, explains it to him, digests it for him so that it doesn't stop in his head but also goes into his heart, and empowers and urges him to put it into practice in his daily living.

In fine, the unbeliever has only a sin nature, so he cannot but sin. He is powerless to consistently say no to sin. The believer has both the old sin nature in him until the Rapture, and also the new nature of the Holy Spirit in him evermore. The believer, then, can and must choose, at each step of his life every day, whom he will choose: the old sinner who died on the cross "in Christ" or the new saint who rose out of death at the empty tomb "in Christ".

King Jesus employs the temptations of the flesh, the world, and the devil, to *test our faith* (verse 2). When a believer fails the test, it is never God's fault. God did His part. He gave the believer the Holy Spirit in him, so that the believer has the power and desire to say no to the temptation. It is the believer's fault. He surrendered to *his own lust* (verse 14) instead of surrendering to the Holy Spirit.

That is the long and short of verses 12-15, brothers and sisters. Then comes verses 16-17, which begin by exhorting the believer to never misunderstand these essential spiritual truths we just restated in the above paragraphs. Every believer must choose whom to follow (cf., Joshua 24:15). Don't let your lust <u>deceive</u> you in this.

And that brings us to verse 17. Let's read it together:

Every good thing given and every perfect gift is from above, coming down from the Father of lights, with whom there is no variation or shifting shadow (verse 17).

A believer falls for a temptation and sins (verse 13). His response is to justify self by blaming God for his sin (verse 13). Not so, says the Holy Spirit. Your own lust is the culprit (verses 14-15).

Then follows verse 16, the ore of which we just finished mining and refining. This verse warns the believer once again not to blame God, but to look in the mirror of God's Word and place the blame squarely on the shoulders of…self: Don't ever be deceived about this, O believer!

That is the **context** for verse 17, brothers and sisters. God is never the cause of any bad thing in the believer's life. Rather, from God comes *every good thing given and every perfect gift*. Satan and sinful man get the credit for the bad stuff. God gets the credit for the good stuff! Spiritual truth 'tis. Why? Because the Bible tells us so. Yes, we know. It's a kid's song. But it's still spiritual truth.

The opening clause of verse 17 (which precedes the comma) at first blush appears to be a redundancy. But it's not! In English it only appears to be because of two items in the translation:

1. every good thing given
2. every perfect gift

Now let's put the corresponding words of each item side-by-side to see how they seem to be synonymous. Each item will appear as Item #1 first, followed by Item #2:

- every vs. every

- good vs. perfect
- thing given vs. gift

A cursory glance screams, "Synonyms all!" But not so, brothers and sisters. Not so. What makes these two items distinct is the last bulleted comparison. The Greek word translated "thing given"—yes, it is one Greek word—is different in meaning from the Greek word translated "gift".

The Greek noun translated "thing given" is *dosis*, from the Greek verb *didomi* (to give). The emphasis is on the act of giving, including the motivation for giving, rather than on the thing which is given. The Greek noun translated "gift" is *dorema*, which emphasizes the thing which is given (aka the "gift" itself).

Each of these two items *comes down from the Father of lights* (verse 17). Consequently, every such "gift", by definition, must be "perfect". Even more, every "act of giving" from *the Father of lights* must be "good". There can be no exceptions to this. <u>Both</u> what is given by *the Father of lights* <u>and</u> His motivation for giving it are above reproach. It is the nature of God—His Person, who He is by definition—to do good always and bad never (as in not ever).

The Greek word translated "good" is *agathos*. The New Testament employs two Greek words which are translated "good":

- *agathos* (the root and vine of what is good)
- *kalos* (the fruit of *agathos*)

In verse 17 of today's text the Greek word used for "good" is *agathos*. When God gives man a "gift", His motivation in doing so (the root and vine which spurs Him to give it) is always "good".

The Greek word translated "perfect" is *teleios*. God creates each person or thing to accomplish his will for it. The more a person or thing grows and matures, so that he/it accomplishes God's will for his/its existence, the more it is "perfect" or "perfected". This word is also translated "complete": he/it becomes increasingly complete as he/it matures. This applies to both a natural world framework and to a spiritual one.

So by His very act of giving (the root and vine, His motivation), God is shown to be "good". In terms of the actual thing given (the gift itself), every such gift is always "perfect". It may not appear to be so at the moment when it is given; but in time (as the gift and/or its recipient mature), the gift is seen as being "perfect" for the person to whom God gives it.

This cannot but be spiritual truth, brothers and sisters. Two proofs for this are furnished in verse 17[b]:

1. the Giver is the Father of lights
2. the Giver has no variation or shifting shadow to Him

The symbolism of light vs. darkness in Scripture is still commonly employed today, so we need not spend much time on it. God began natural creation (Genesis 1) by speaking it into existence.

The first thing we learn is that it was a lot of raw material, which was piled in a humongous heap and covered in <u>darkness</u>. So God began forming this raw material into a finished product by speaking <u>light</u> into existence. That makes sense. Right? Who wants to work in the dark? We want to see what we are doing, after all.

Now God is Spirit, so He needs no physical "light" by which to see. That isn't the point. In Scripture God employs visible physical realities of time and space, so as to teach man the invisible spiritual truths of eternity. We can't understand eternity because we have never been there. Oh, and in our natural state we are not equipped to understand eternity either. Like kids, we need picture stories.

That is the point. The light wasn't created so God could see. It was created so man and animals could see, and so plants could grow. Ergo, before creating man and animals and plants, God followed His perfect plan of creation. It was orderly, logical, as demonstrated, for instance, by creating light before creating anything else.

Yes, God did create all of the raw materials for creation, light excepted, before creating the light. And yes, He could've created the light first, or simultaneously with the raw materials of physical creation. The fact that He didn't is to teach man *invisible spiritual* truth. So let's consider what the invisible spiritual truth is for God doing so.

It teaches us that natural creation is darkness without the light of God. God's Word is a lamp to our feet and a light to our path (cf., Psalm 119:105). The new heaven and new earth, which God will create after the Millennium, will have no sun or moon to provide it with light. God Himself will be the light for this new creation (cf., Revelation 21:22-27).

This speaks volumes about the loud assertions of "science" in the atheistic world of unbelievers today. The nomenclature "science" is defined as that which man can see with his eyes. Consider the axiom, "If I can't see it, I don't believe it!" This sorry excuse for "science" depends solely on the natural creation, you see.

This is why, at the very start of His Word, in the first few words, God created the raw materials of natural creation without light. Without God Himself and His Word (the light), natural creation can never suffice in bringing man true and complete knowledge. True "science" (aka knowledge) is never at odds with God's Word.

God created all things. This makes Him the "Father" of all things. This spiritual truth itself is also illustrated in Genesis 1. Where did

God get the raw materials for forming the natural creation? Answer: God said…and it was so. Everything came from God. In natural creation this is symbolized by the birthing process. The raw materials of creation, and the light, came from God's Word alone: the physical fetus who is birthed into a baby comes from ma and pa alone.

Of course all of this goes back to God as providing ma and pa with the semen and the egg. But on the natural plane, ma and pa need not go to the store to purchase any additional raw materials, in order to have a baby. This is the sense given by the description of God as *the Father of lights*.

It is also significant that Pastor James wrote to Jewish believers who lived in the Gentile lands (aka the *diaspora*). Back in the day those areas of the world were rife with what we now know as the *Mystery Religions*, of which *Gnosticism* was the most common.

In these false religions, the theme of "light vs. darkness" is standard fare. Any talk about "God" had to revolve around equating "good" with "light" vs. "bad or evil" with "darkness". In that **context** Pastor James teaches his audience that <u>both</u> sinning <u>and</u> blaming God = darkness because God is the *Father of lights*.

Additionally, *there is no variation or shifting shadow* with God. This means that God never varies. He is always the same. In terms of the light vs. darkness theme, God is never a "shifting shadow".

Didn't God favor the <u>nation</u> of Israel at one time, and later dispatch them out of the Promised Land and into exile in Babylon? Yep, He sure enough did that. Then God does change (or have "variation"). Uh, that would be a no, as Pastor James just said in verse 17.

There are two relevant details for us to consider vis-à-vis this topic. First, when God sent the Israelites into exile, He didn't change. He told them ahead of time—and even recorded it in His Word so they wouldn't forget it—that, should they stop serving Him as their King, He would do just what He did. Ergo, there was no change on God's part. The change was on the part of the Israelites. They swore to serve only King Yahveh (aka the "Lord"). They broke their oath, and in consequence received from God exactly what He swore to them He would do, should they ever break His oath.

Secondly, God is the perfect Father (as in Father of lights, verse 17). He is our role model, parents. When Sonny Boy is good, we praise him up to encourage him to persist in being good. When Sonny Boy ceases to be good and does bad, we paddle his little behind to encourage him to cease doing bad. What's the matter with us? Why did we change? We didn't...but Sonny Boy did!

God is Light, and in Him there is no darkness at all [1 John 1:5]. That is Point #1 of our list above. Additionally,

> *For I, the Lord, do not change; therefore you, O sons of Jacob, are not consumed* [Malachi 3:6].

That is Point #2 of our list above. Throughout the *Book of Malachi*, God exposes the many sins of the Israelites of Malachi's day. And yet God didn't utterly exterminate them for their sins. Why not? Answer: because *I, the Lord, do not change*. In the words of Pastor James, *There is no variation or shifting shadow* with God.

God pledged to Abraham, and to his progeny who followed him, many unconditional promises. If God failed to fulfill even one of those promises, then there would be "variation" with Him. There would be "shifting" with Him. But this can never be. This is why the <u>nation</u> of Israel will still return to God and receive Jesus as their Messiah at the conclusion of the Tribulation Period. This is why Jesus will be their King and restore them to the Promised Land for a Millennium. He will fulfill the Abrahamic Covenant.

> *In the exercise of His will He brought us forth by the word*
> *of truth, so that we would be a kind of first fruits among*
> *His creatures* (verse 18).

(Sounds an awful lot like Paul. Anyway, we digress.) God doesn't tempt His people to do evil. He does use temptations to help His people mature. But whenever His people are tempted and do evil in consequence, God isn't the culprit! The believer who does evil is. His own lust got him in the mess he is in, the evil he sampled.

Quite the contrary, everything good—and in the **context** of James' letter, "good" as used here is the opposite of all things "evil"—but everything "good" for the believer comes from God. The contrast is between "bad" (or "evil") which comes from the believer's own lust vs. "good" (or "righteous") which comes from God.

The believer can depend on God for deliverance in temptation because God is "light". Also, He never changes (as in "varies" or "shifts"). As light God reveals the way for us to take, as we walk with Him through life. As never changing, God doesn't say one thing one minute and a different thing the next. The believer can learn God's ways and live His life, without ever having to second-guess Him and what He wants from the believer.

That is the context in which verse 18 is to be interpreted, brothers and sisters. God exerted His will, and "the word of truth" came forth. What was God's will in the context of James 1:2-17? Oh, that's simple, silly billy. He gives us His Word ("the word of truth"), so that…

Stop! Don't take another step! "So that" is an infinitive in the Greek, and it is quite accurate. It announces that what follows is God's purpose for what precedes it. Verse 18[a] teaches that God "brought believers forth"; then in verse 18[b] the reason for God "bringing the believer forth" is stated. Let's investigate further.

The Greek verb translated "brought us forth" occurs twice in the New Testament, both times in the *Book of James*. The first time is in James 1:15, where we are taught that sin "brings forth" death. The second time is obviously right here in verse 18.

In Scripture the contrast is made with regularity between sin and death vs. righteousness and life. In verse 16 this Greek word is used of the first contrast ("sin resulting in death"). It would seem reasonable to see this Greek word in verse 18 being used in terms of the second contrast ("righteousness and life").

This Greek word was actually used back in the day as "bringing forth" in terms of childbirth. Sin gives birth to death, righteousness gives birth to life. Ezekiel prophesied, *The soul that sins shall die* (cf., Ezekiel 18:20). Sin gives birth to death, you see. *But the righteous man will live by his faith* (cf., Habakkuk 2:4; Hebrews 10:38). Righteousness gives birth to life.

That makes verse 18[a] quite explicit, which provides us with clarity as we interpret verse 18[b]. God birthed the believer = rebirth or being born again (verse 18[a]); and He had a purpose, His purpose, for doing so. His purpose is that believers *be a kind of first fruits among His creatures.*

> *Huh? I thought you said we had clarity now, teacher. That isn't clear to me!*

The clarity was in verse 18[a], dear sister, clarity to help us interpret verse 18[b]. We are now in verse 18[b], so its meaning won't become clear until we finish interpreting it. A thousand pardons for the confusion, ma'am.

Oh, dear. We are out of time today, so you will have to remain unclear until tomorrow. Or maybe if you give it to Jesus, He will make it clear. That's good spiritual exercise. Why not try it?

James 1:18-19

Clarity vs. confusion. That was the issue when we paused our last study. We sincerely hope your dreams were not confused too! Let's get right to today's study and disperse the fog in our noggins. We will begin by reading the verse again.

In the exercise of His will He brought us forth by the word of truth, so that we would be a kind of first fruits among His creatures (verse 18).

Verse 18^a is now clear to us. God ("the Father", verse 17) rebirthed us for His own purpose. This means no one is born again so that he can continue to seek his own will and purpose in life. Believers are rebirthed so they can learn God's purpose for him personally, and then put God's purpose into practice.

This cannot be accomplished, so long as the believer wants his own way in life, e.g., the wife he chooses, the location where he will live, the occupation at which he will work, the church he will attend, etc. Give them all to Jesus, and He will lift you up to victorious Christian living, brothers and sisters.

We have slogans and catchwords aplenty in church. For example,

- Jesus is Lord! – but we don't let Him rule our life
- I am serving Jesus – while not knowing His individual, personal will for us

All such concepts are contradictions! How is it we don't seem to fathom that God recreated us ("rebirth") for His purpose, not for our own purpose?

Suppose you instruct your teenage son to be sure to be home Saturday afternoon, telling him that you need him to help you do something. Come Saturday afternoon and he is nowhere to be found. When you see him that evening, you challenge him about it. He seriously and innocently responds, "Dad, I was in the garage cleaning it up for you. You should say thank you to me, not get on my case!" Would you respond by saying thank you to him? Fat chance of that!

Let's each of us be honest <u>with</u> <u>self</u> for a moment, all churchiness aside. Isn't that what often transpires in our concept of "serving Jesus"? Don't we tend to see behaving a certain way and doing certain things as "serving Jesus". Why doesn't it seem to occur to the believer to wonder what Jesus wants him personally to do for Him? Could it be that this concept isn't addressed from the pulpit?

God rebirthed us for <u>His</u> purpose, not our own, O believer. A person's own purpose = the old life of sin. It lives by "Thus saith me!" God's purpose in a believer's life = the new life of Christ living in me (cf., Galatians 2:20). It goes by "Thus saith the Lord!"

The *Book of James* is a letter written to Jewish believers who live in Gentile lands (aka the *diaspora*), as opposed to the land of the Jews (aka the Promised Land). As such, it does not address any believers on an individual basis, in order to tell them what God's will for them is personally. For that matter, nowhere in the entire Bible is such a revelation to be found.

Then where is the believer to discover God's will for His life personally? Answer: well, since we are talking individual, personal matters between God and the believer, the answer will come from God on an individual, personal basis. Ergo, the believer learns God's will for him personally by being alone with Jesus. He must,

> *Establish a spiritual regimen of daily quiet time alone with Jesus, Bible open and man's books closed, with hands folded in prayer.*

That is how a believer avoids mimicking common church practices for how to "serve Jesus", but instead does God's will for his life personally.

Two Greek words in verse 18[b] are crucial for us to comprehend, if we would rightly interpret the verse. The two are,

- *aparche* ("first fruits")
- *ktisma* ("creatures")

Point #1: *aparche* (first fruits). The concept of "first fruits" derives from *Torah* (aka the Law of Moses). Yahveh (aka the Lord God) was the Israelites' King. He gave them the Promised Land as their earthly territory in which to live. He gave them *Torah* (i.e., their legal code to govern them as they lived in their land).

As it is with every nation, there are the citizens on one hand, and the governing authority (or authorities) on the other. In the case of the <u>nation</u> of Israel, the Israelites were the citizenry and King Yahveh was the governing authority. King Yahveh established the adult males of the tribe of Levi to be His government officials, and the family of Aaron in the tribe of Levi to be His chief officials.

The Israelites never had a vote on whom they wanted to be their king, or who would be the government officials. Even when they finally demanded a human king, King Yahveh gave them His choice. First He gave them Saul, a man after the people's own heart. Secondly He gave them David, a man after God's own heart.

Yahveh (the Lord God), you see, was still their King. He did the choosing and they did the serving. In the same vein the Israelites paid taxes to King Yahveh. This consisted of giving Him a *tithe* every year. The word *tithe* is Hebrew for "one-tenth". So we mustn't see it as one certain object or thing. It is a measurement. In the case of the Law it is a measurement of the Israelite's wealth.

Torah called for two *tithes* every year, plus a third *tithe* every third year (aka "the year of the tithe"). This amounts to 23⅓% of their wealth paid in taxes. Plus they gave freewill offerings of all sorts as they saw fit, all because they loved King Yahveh.

That is not exactly the pretty picture we are taught in most churches today is it, brothers and sisters. Believers are prone to think that they can give one-tenth of their income to God, and heaven's ledger marks them paid-in-full. They have met their responsibilities to God. He must be so pleased with them.

Yikes! Now that we know better, let us be done with all of the talk about "paying our *tithes*". Instead, let us spiritually mature into discovering God's will for our life individually. It doesn't consist of a set of dos and don'ts, but of cultivating a personal relationship with King Jesus, which we do by,

> *Establishing a spiritual regimen of daily quiet time alone with Jesus, Bible open and man's books closed, with hands folded in prayer.*

The taxes the Israelites paid were to be done on the basis of the "first fruits" (cf., Proverbs 3:9-10). This statute of the Law taught that King Yahveh deserved the first and the best of each Israelite's wealth.

In other words, as he paid his taxes to the government, the Israelite couldn't take the sick and lame and weakling animals of his herds and flocks as the King's portion, while reserving the best of the lot for himself. The first and the best was King Yahveh's portion. Sounds like our government today requiring that the first portion of the employee's pay be deducted from their paycheck!

That was the concept of the "first fruits", brothers and sisters. All things are created by God, so all things belong to God. We mere humans don't give Him anything: He gives us whatever we have! By giving some of what we have, we acknowledge that all of our livelihood comes from Him. By giving Him the first and the best, we take it one step further and acknowledge that He deserves our very best, not our leftovers.

The Apostle Paul identifies Christ Jesus as the "first fruits". Let's hear Brother Paul tell it:

But now Christ has been raised from the dead, the first fruits of those who are asleep [1 Corinthians 15:20].

Note the **context** there. Christ is the "first fruits" as being the first person to be raised out of death. *Those who are asleep*, then, are those who are <u>dead</u>. Christ physically rose out of death, so *those who are asleep* are those who are <u>physically</u> <u>dead</u>.

The Apostle Paul then takes this concept further in verses 21-23, which concludes thusly:

...in Christ all will be made alive. But each in his own order: Christ the first fruits, after that those who are Christ's at His coming [1 Corinthians 15:22-23].

Torah's concept of the first fruits is applied <u>spiritually</u> to the resurrection of the dead. The Israelites literally, <u>physically</u>, planted seeds in the ground. The seeds grew into crops for their food. They acknowledged King Yahveh's provision for them by giving Him the "first fruits", the first and the best of what He gave them.

God "planted" man on the earth. All men belong to Him, as do all things. Mankind sinned against God by disobeying His Word to them, so they died physically. They also died spiritually, which means they became separated from God. God and man no longer had a personal relationship.

As sinners, men are incapable of making things right with God and mending their relationship with Him. After all, no one can make chicken salad out of chicken feathers. Sinners sin. They don't live righteously. But living righteously is what *Torah* (aka the Law of Moses) required, in order to have a relationship with God. How "righteous" must man be. Listen to Jesus tell it:

> *Therefore you are to be perfect, as your heavenly Father is perfect* [Matthew 5:48].

Yikes! Sinful man must not just get his act together and be nicer than he is. He must be absolutely PERFECT! So that we don't misunderstand what this means, Messiah Jesus spells it out for us in plain-speak: we must be as perfect as Father God is.

This creates a great divide between God and sinful man, one only God can fix. So He did! He sent His only begotten Son to become a real flesh-and-blood human male, so that He could fulfill all righteousness on man's behalf (cf., Matthew 3:15), and then to die to pay the penalty for man's sins, which is death.

And this brings us back to our text for today, having to do with the concept of the "first fruits". As the Apostle Paul taught us,

> *...in Christ all will be made alive. But each in his own order: Christ the first fruits, after that those who are Christ's at His coming* [1 Corinthians 15:22-23].

Torah (aka the Law of Moses) applied this to the <u>visible physical realities</u> of the Israelites' lives back in the day. The Lord God did so in order to teach man the <u>invisible spiritual truths</u> of eternity. In other words all of *Tanakh* (aka the Old Testament) serves as God's prophecies of spiritual truths (cf., Luke 24:44), fulfilled in the New Testament under the Covenant of Grace, as well as during the Millennium and the new heaven and new earth which follow.

What are the spiritual truths we are to learn about the concept of the "first fruits"? Just this. Christ Jesus is the "first fruits" from the dead. Those who accept Him as their sin offering, and are born again thereby, are the spiritual crops which follow (cf., Romans 8:23; 16:5).

By virtue of being "in Christ", we share His death on the cross as the payment for the penalty of our sins. We also share His physical resurrection for our *justification*, and rise out of death into newness of life "in Him" (cf., Romans 4:25). This means that, "in Christ", every believer is also the "first fruits" of the dead, just as Christ is.

A kind of first fruits. The qualifier "a kind of" is used to distinguish believers from Messiah Jesus (aka *Christ*). He is the first human being who, having died for sins, rose out of death without sin. That is what makes Jesus' death and resurrection unique from those who were raised out of death before Him.

Yes, "in Christ" we believers share His resurrection out of death with Him. But we are not Him! He is unique. We are "a kind of" first fruits vicariously (i.e., "in Him" as our substitute sin offering). The true and only "first fruits" is Messiah Jesus, but we share this position with Him as "a kind of" the real deal.

Point #2: *ktisma* (creatures). The Greek word derives from the verb *ktizo* (to create). As a noun it means "created things" (aka "creatures"). Let's not succumb to contemporary Syfy images of swamp "creatures" out to steal people's lives! Any person or thing in all of "creation" is a "creature" (a created person or thing).

Among all of God's creation, Christ Jesus is the "first fruits" by virtue of being the first to die for sins—man's sins, not His own, but with sins on Him nonetheless—and still rise out of death with no sins any longer needing judged. He is first, and "in Him" we believers share His first fruits (His first place trophy) with Him!

Of all creation we are the first to hold this exalted position. But again, we are not the origin or source of being first fruits. Only Christ is. We are His Body, the Church; and as such we are the first fruits by virtue of being "in Him".

And that is where verse 18 of our text comes into play in our study of the concept of the "first fruits", brothers and sisters. Let's recap this section of the text succinctly.

- God doesn't sin or cause man to sin (verse 13)
- sin (all bad things) is man's doing (verses 14-15)
- all good things are God's doing (verses 16-17)
- God wills it, and so it is that we are born again, a good thing (verse 18).

Now we can move on to the next section of the text.

This you know, my beloved brethren. But everyone must be quick to hear, slow to speak and slow to anger (verse 19).

Again we have Pastor James' preferred phrase for believers: *my beloved brethren*. "Brethren" = Christians or believers. "Beloved" = those "loved" (aka *agape*) by God. The cherry on top of the sundae = "my": James makes them "his" siblings in the Family of God. And such it is for all of us too. Each of us should view other believers as our spiritual siblings. As such we will spend eternity together; it may be wisdom for us to get use to each other now!

This you know. In the Greek it is one word (*iste*, from *eidon*), a perfect tense imperative (a command). It has the sense, "You once learned this and still know it", but in the sense of a command. Once upon a time they were born again. They learned of their sin (the source of all bad) and Christ's salvation (the source of all good). You learned it then; continuously keep it fresh in the mind!

The reason why believers should do so is that they are brethren, siblings in the Family of God. As such they have God's love (*agape*). With God living in each of us believers, we should have *agape* for each other too.

That is the sense of the opening words in verse 19. We can already gather from this that a new section of the text has just begun. These few opening words of verse 19 connect what follows with what came before in the prior section.

What is the theme of this new section of the text? Answer: the latter part of verse 19 identifies it for us:

> *...But everyone must be quick to hear, slow to speak and slow to anger* (verse 19[b]).

The theme is this: when facing trials or struggles in life, bite your tongue and meditate on the Word of truth. The wrong behavior in this new section (verses 19-27) is sinful man's tongue. No, not how he uses it to eat, silly goose, but how it is the source of his words. And contrary to the old adage about sticks and stones vs. words, yes, words most certainly can, and do, hurt us!

Everyone. The literal Greek reads "every man" (*pas anthropos*). But no, Pastor James didn't change his audience. He doesn't mean "everyone", as in the entire world…though his teaching would benefit every human being. The **context** is *my beloved brethren* (believers).

Here's the thing about good works and right behaviors, brothers and sisters. Sinners cannot do them! Certainly they can't, if we are talking about good works and right behaviors in God's eyes. Why not? Answer: because no one can make chicken salad out of chicken feathers. Sinners sin. They don't live righteously. They cannot do good works and behave righteously.

What this means for the Church is that we don't spend our time trying to teach sinners not to sin. We point them to Jesus to be saved. Jesus saves: we don't. When a sinner is born again (aka *justification*), then the job of the Church (us believers) is to rear them to spiritual maturity (aka *sanctification*). But it is pouring water into a leaky cistern, to try and stop sinners from sinning and to live righteously. First they must become saints via rebirth.

Everyone must be… The Greek verb translated "must be" is a present tense imperative. Hence the translation "must". It's a command, not a good suggestion. We might phrase it as "every believer must continuously be".

The command involves three aspects. These are,

1. quick to hear
2. slow to speak
3. slow to anger

These three subdivide into two other sets of three. These are,

- quick, slow, slow
- hear, speak, anger

Oh, dear me. Time has flown the coop. We will have to take our leave of y'all, my beloved brethren. (Brother James is wearing off on me.)

But not to fret. Jesus is always available day or night. The sign on His door (the prayer closet) reads, "The doctor is in." Yep, like with Lucy on the Peanuts cartoon. So just betake yourself to His office and have yourself a splendid time of fellowship with Him. We'll meet back here on the morrow.

James 1:19-21

We concluded our last study at verse 19. We still have the second part of the verse to finish. We noted that the Greek verb translated "must be" is a present imperative, making it a command to be obeyed continuously.

We observed how the command involves three aspects. These are,

1. quick to hear
2. slow to speak
3. slow to anger

These three subdivide into of two other sets of three:

-   quick, slow, slow
-   hear, speak, anger

We will now take up our study from there. Let us begin by reading the verse once more, to plant it fresh in our mind:

This you know, my beloved brethren. But everyone must be quick to hear, slow to speak and slow to anger (verse 19).

Aspect #1: quick to hear. Each of these three behaviors have to do with believers spiritually maturing. The three aspects are fruit of spiritual maturity. Let us keep this in mind, lest we see it as <u>being</u> saved (*justification*). It's not; it is <u>living</u> <u>as</u> saved (*sanctification*).

The Greek verb is the standard verb used in the New Testament for "to hear". However, in the **context** of the Scriptures, the concept of "hearing" is to "listen" and then attend to what we hear. In the case of the Word of God, we are to focus on it (i.e., listen as God speaks to us). That is the first step, but there is another. After we take in what God tells us, we respond by putting it into practice in our life.

In the **context** of doing this, we are commanded to continuously do it (present tense imperative "must be"). The believer is to be in a ready state at all times to hear God's voice. Hence the translation "quick".

The Greek adjective translated "quick" is *tachus*. We get our English word *tachometer* from it (tacho + meter). A tachometer in a car or airplane measures the "speed" (i.e., the "quickness") of the vehicle. It does so by measuring the RPMs (revolutions per second) of the engine.

Ergo, our English word is not a *translation* but a *transliteration*. A *translation* replaces the Greek word with an English word which means the same thing. A *transliteration* keeps the Greek word and changes the Greek letters to English letters which sound the same.

Remember the context for verse 19, viz., verses 2-18. Jesus said that the believer will have tribulation in the world (cf., John 16:33). When he does, he is to seek instructions from God for how to proceed, not follow the method of the flesh by handling things in his own power—which is to be slow to hear God's Word and quick to verbalize whatever emotions are aroused by the tribulation.

That is the context. No bad thing is from God: every good thing is. God's love (aka *agape*) for the believer surrounds him in all things always. Consequently, the believer should respond to any and every trial by walking in the Spirit.

This is aspect #1 of our text, viz., "quick to hear (or listen)". It is how the Spirit in us responds to trials and tribulations in life. When the believer responds to stimuli in his life in that fashion, he is walking in the Spirit. The flipside of the coin is aspect #2.

Aspect #2: slow to speak. The Greek verb translated "speak" is the usual New Testament word for "speak". When a believer is the one doing the speaking, what is said is expected to be God's Word. This is especially true when dealing with trials and tribulation in his life. Even more, when a believer speaks God's Word, he must not simply state the words. He must speak the truth in love (cf., Ephesians 4:15).

God's Word = the truth (cf., John 17:17). Messiah Jesus = the truth (cf., John 14:6). This tells us that we learn how to speak God's Word "in love" by observing in Scripture how Jesus did it. What we learn is that sometimes speaking the truth in love is sweet and gentle encouragement, at other times harsh rebuke.

By reading of the Gospel accounts of Jesus' life, we learn that those to whom Jesus spoke God's Word determined whether Jesus came with gentleness or rebuke. Those who heard the former (i.e., gentleness) were the weak and needy. They sought Jesus because they wanted Him.

Those who heard the latter (i.e., rebuke) were those in the church building (or the temple and synagogues). They thought they already knew God's Word, so they challenged Jesus' authority so as to promote their own authority. To them Jesus was expected to come to church and fit in with their rituals and leadership. But they didn't follow God's Word at all. They followed the interpretations of mere men (the rabbis), which replaced God's Word.

In the first classification of folks, they were "quick to listen" and "slow to speak". This portrays people who want to hear what God says to them, so that they may get right with God. In the second classification of folks, they were the exact opposite. They already knew (or so they said) what God's Word taught; so they were quick to speak and slow to listen.

Aspect #3: slow to anger. The Greek word translated "anger" is at times translated "wrath". We mustn't limit it to one meaning, but allow the **context** to determine which definition to use in each case. The Greek word is *orge*. The action (the outward expression of anger) isn't the main thing. The source of the action is; and this comes from inside the believer. Jesus' anger came from *agape*.

As a believer matures spiritually, he is increasingly conformed to the image of Jesus. This means he thinks and speaks and acts like Jesus. This isn't an outward spitting image. The believer still has the personality God gave him at conception and birth. But his motivation is based on the Word of God, as he hides God's Word in his heart so that he doesn't sin against God.

Jesus role modeled for the believer how to live. He laid aside His prerogatives as God and took upon true humanity (cf., Philippians 2:5-8). This means that, though Jesus is always God, He became a real flesh and blood human male and lived that way. He didn't exercise His powers as God. Instead, He fed on the Word of God and walked in the Spirit, depending on the Word of God to lead Him, as the Spirit taught it to Him and empowered Him to obey it.

That is how you and I and every believer are expected to live. Any other approach to "serving Jesus" is no better than sinful man in religious garb, as he does what is right in his own eyes and thinks God is pleased. But doing what is right in our own eyes is the definition of sin! It is to eat fruit from the **kogae tree** (man's words) rather than from the **life tree** (God's Word).

The application of verse 19 is twofold because the *Book of James* is twofold. We learned in the prior portion of chapter 1 that in the world believers will have tribulation (or "trials"; verse 2).

In this letter Pastor James addresses many other issues, which have to do with the interaction between believers inside the Church. We just applied the text to the believer as he interacts with the world. Now let's apply it to believers as they interact with each other.

God is "love" (aka *agape*). Agape (God's love) gives to others. It doesn't take from others as man's "love" (aka *philia*) does. Any person who is truly born again has the Holy Spirit inside Him. We will let y'all in on a secret, but you must promise to tell everybody. Father God and Son God (Jesus) also live inside the believer.

Seeing how God (Father, Son, and Holy Spirit) is *agape*, believers are also to spiritually mature to where we no longer function based on *philia* (seeking our own good), but instead function based on *agape* (seeking the good of others, and especially those of the household of God (cf., Galatians 6:10).

We just learned how Jesus functioned as our role model. He was gentle to little lambs who sought out the Shepherd and followed Him. He rebuked the goats who promoted man's words over God's Word in the assembly of believers.

In both cases Jesus spoke the truth "in love" (aka *agape*). We tend to think of "love" as peaceful and gentle. We interpret this by how things affect us. If we don't like something, it isn't love. If it pleases us, then it is love.

But without a rebuke, the goats—in Jesus' case the Pharisees and scribes, the Sadducees and Herodians—would never repent, and their blood would be on the believer's head because he didn't sound the alarm, so that the goat could be offered the opportunity to repent (cf., Ezekiel 33:1-6).

God desires that all men be saved and come to a knowledge of the truth (cf., 1 Timothy 2:4). Whatever it takes to snatch a burning ember from the fire—gentleness, rebuke, and all in-between—if it brings a person to repentance and rebirth, it births *agape*. Use it!

> *...for the anger of man does not achieve the righteousness of God* (verse 20).

Prior to verse 19 a believer's individual behaviors and habits aren't addressed. His response to "trials", to struggles in life, are the topic. He is taught that God isn't to blame for these realities of life. Sin is, and sin is in us believers as well as in the unbelievers.

In all of these struggles of life, though God isn't the origin of evil, He is still on His throne. He makes use of the evil to accomplish His own purposes (cf., Genesis 50:20). All bad comes from sin and sinners. All good comes from God. The believer's salvation "in Christ" is a good thing, so it comes from God. He chose each and every believer to be *a kind of first fruits among His creatures* (verse 18; cf., Romans 8:19).

That is the **context** for verses 19-20, brothers and sisters. Observe in your Bible how the first part of verse 19 is a separate sentence with a period at the end of it. It's the same in the original Greek text too. We read the text as verse 19[a] applying to verses 12-18.

> *All bad comes from sin. All good comes from God. This you know!* (our paraphrase—R.G.)

Then follows the new section of the text, beginning with verse 19[b]. Verse 19[a], then, serves to connect the section about all bad things being sin's doing and all good things being God's, with the section about the tongue out of control (a bad thing) vs. the tongue under God's control (a good thing).

If the believer keeps recalling (as per verse 19[a]) the spiritual truth of verses 2-18 (bad = sin, good = God), then he will recognize that his out-of-control tongue is a bad thing (i.e., sin), so it is not from God. Recognition of sin is the first step to repenting and being restored into fellowship with God and His people.

That is the **context** of our text for today. If we keep recalling it, we will grasp the spiritual truths available to us in the text.

Verse 19 introduces the first specifically outward action of sin in a believer's life, which he must learn to control. Control in a believer comes from the Holy Spirit, as He teaches the believer the Word of God, wherein all spiritual truth is to be learned. As Rule #2 for Bible study teaches,

> *The Bible is our sole and final authority in all matters of faith and practice.*

The believer is a new creation "in Christ". He is a <u>spiritual</u> being. Ergo, all thoughts, words, and deeds for the believer should be spiritual (cf., 1 John 2:1). Behaviors are the fruit of the person (the root and vine). Spiritual person = spiritual fruit. When the fruit is not spiritual (aka from Christ as per the Word of God), then the flesh is in control of the believer at that moment (cf., 1 John 2:2[a]).

This is where verse 19 comes into Pastor James' letter. Automatic responses of the tongue to external stimuli results in sin. Keep the tongue under control, O believer! Don't rashly utter your opinion about things, the moment you are confronted by them.

Rather, be quick to listen and slow to speak; then you will be slow to anger over those things. Recall the Word of God about such things, and allow His Word to interpret the stimuli. The flesh already knows it all, so it is automatically riled over what it doesn't like, and tells everyone so too!

The Spirit, contrariwise, keeps the tongue under control, calmly expressing God's "opinion" of the stimuli. This eliminates fleshly anger, while allowing God's anger to come forth as He deems fit.

That is the contrast we witness in verse 20:

- the anger of man (aka the flesh)
- the righteousness of God (aka the Spirit)

The "anger" of man is distinct from man's "wrath". Anger (Greek = *orge*) originates from an established propensity inside a person. His thoughts concerning certain stimuli are consciously thought out, and his response to it follows from that. Wrath (Greek = *thumos*), on the other hand, is an automatic reflex, a passionate outburst which abruptly results from some stimuli or other.

The issue in verses 19-20, then, is about the bad habits of the old sinner. The unbeliever has these, and they control him because he has nothing else inside to control him. The believer, however, has the Holy Spirit living inside him. The believer is to spiritually mature to the point where he responds to the Spirit rather than to the flesh (aka *walking in the Spirit* vs. *walking in the flesh*).

The original Greek text of verse 20 literally reads,

> *For the anger of man the righteousness of God does not work* (verse 20, literal).

Man's anger comes first in the clause, you see. This means it receives the emphasis. Since verses 19 and 20 are one sentence, this tells us the emphasis for verse 19 is also man's anger, and specifically as it stands in stark contrast to God's righteousness.

The concept of "righteousness" has to do with what is "right". Our opinion about what is "right" depends on whom we accept as the judge of all things. The believer knows that the Judge of all things is God, so he follows Rule #2 for Bible study which we quoted on the prior page. (The Bible is our sole and final authority at all times and for every circumstance!)

Righteousness = doing right as God defines it. Sin = doing wrong as God defines it (doing what God says don't do and not doing what God says to do). Take a read of Genesis 2-3, and pay careful attention to the theme of the **life tree** vs. the **kogae tree**.

Consider how this concept fits into the *Book of James*. In verse 5 the believer is instructed about how to handle "various trials" (verse 2). Verse 5 directs the believer to "ask God" for the answer. That is the definition of prayer. In verse 13 the believer is warned about blaming God, when he fails to ask God what to do about a temptation and so he sins as a result.

Do you see how all of this fits together? Waddaya mean no? Whew, boy. You are a tough bunch. It's like this. A believer's anger is the flesh in action. That is the meaning of "the anger of man". It is in stark contrast to "the anger of the Spirit". That is why the phrase "the righteousness of God" follows on the heels of the phrase "the anger of man". The two phrases are put in contrast to each other: man vs. God & anger vs. righteousness.

In verse 19 the believer receives a caveat about the necessity to listen a lot and speak a little, lest he lose control to the flesh and be angry a lot. That is a paraphrase of verse 19. Then verse 20 (the same sentence, remember) goes on to address the same "anger" as was introduced in verse 19. Verse 19 introduces "anger" by its first name (Anger), and verse 20 introduces him by his first, middle, and last name (Anger of Man). They are one and the same, even as Pharaoh's two dreams were (cf., Genesis 41:25).

> *Therefore, putting aside all filthiness and all that remains of wickedness, in humility receive the word implanted, which is able to save your souls* (verse 21).

Rule #3 for Bible study teaches,

> *Whenever you see the word "therefore" in Scripture, stop and determine what it is there for.*

Okay. We'll bite. What is the reason for the word "therefore" to appear at this juncture of the text, O God? Answer: the word "therefore" connects what precedes it with what follows. There. We said it. Whew. That is a load off our shoulders.

What precedes the word "therefore" is what we just learned about the anger of man vs. the righteousness of God. Man's anger = bad, and bad = sin. God's righteousness = good because God is the Judge of all things and he says it is good.

That is what precedes the word "therefore" in verse 21. This word basically states, "Now here is what follows, based on what just preceded it." Okay, then what follows? Duh! We just read it a handful of paragraphs prior, silly goose. Listen this time:

> *...putting aside all filthiness and all that remains of wickedness, in humility receive the word implanted, which is able to save your souls* (verse 21).

That is what follows the word "therefore" in verse 21. Keeping the text in **context**, we understand that, seeing how man's anger = the flesh and is bad, and seeing how God's righteousness = the Spirit and is good, what follows in verse 21 continues the same theme. Ergo, we should expect verse 21 to present some examples of "the anger of man" (from which the believer is to be cleansed), and conversely examples of "the righteousness of God" (which the believer is to substitute in place of the wrong examples).

Now reread verse 21 as quoted above. Is that not exactly what we find? Yes, it is; but we will have to wait for the morrow to show how this is so because we are out of time today. Enjoy a time of refreshing with Jesus now. Chew the cud on what we learned in today's study, and ask the Spirit to copy it from your head and paste it in your heart.

James 1:21-22

I n our last study we noted the word "therefore" at the start of verse 21. This word announces that what follows is connected to what precedes it.

Keeping the text in **context** in this manner, we understand that, seeing how man's anger = the flesh and is bad, and seeing how God's righteousness = the Spirit and is good (all of which precedes the word "therefore"), what follows in verse 21 continues the same theme. Ergo, we should expect verse 21 to present some examples of "the anger of man" (from which the believer is to be cleansed), and conversely examples of "the righteousness of God" (which the believer is to substitute in place of the wrong examples).

Now let's reread verse 21 and see if this is in fact the case.

> *Therefore, putting aside all filthiness and all that remains of wickedness, in humility receive the word implanted, which is able to save your souls* (verse 21).

Well, waddaya know. Verse 21 does indeed afford us examples of what precedes it. We guess Rule #3 for Bible study is an accurate rule after all. We will restate this rule one more time here for the record. It teaches,

> *Whenever you see the word "therefore" in Scripture, stop and determine what it is there for.*

The word "therefore" at the start of verse 21 announces that the theme of what precedes it in the *Book of James* is continued in verse 21. What does precede it? Answer: the anger of man vs. the righteousness of God. Man's anger = bad, and bad = sin. God's righteousness = good because God is the Judge of all things, and He says it is good (our paraphrase of verses 2-20).

Verse 21 then follows to provide examples of these spiritual truths. On one hand is God, on the other is man. God is righteous, man is sinful. When God is angry—and He often is because His creation disobeys Him at every turn!—God's anger is righteous because He is righteous, and cannot but be so always. When man is angry, his anger is sinful because man is sinful, and cannot but be so always.

While still on this earth, the believer (an erstwhile sinful man) still walks this earth of sin bedecked in his old body of sin. He will continue in this state until his *glorification* at the Rapture, when he will receive his eternal spiritual body like Jesus has been wearing since His own resurrection.

This separates believers from unbelievers. Unbelievers have only a sin nature, so they cannot but sin. After all, no one can make chicken salad out of chicken feathers. Sinners sin. They don't live righteously.

The believer, contrariwise, continues to have <u>both</u> the old sinful nature (his body of sin) <u>and</u> the new nature of the Holy Spirit living in him. This leaves him with a choice to make at every turn. He is continuously tempted to sin (cf., verses 2-4, 13-18). Will he succumb to the temptation by listening to the old sin nature in him? Or will he instead heed the Holy Spirit and resist the temptation?

The believer, you see, has a left foot that still tries to walk in the world of sin, while the right foot chooses to walk in the Kingdom of God. This requires him to continuously, increasingly mature spiritually, so that he allows his right foot to do the leading—or rather the Holy Spirit to lead the right foot on the path of life.

Verse 21 affords us examples of the left foot vs. the right foot:

1. not putting aside all filthiness (left foot)
2. not putting aside…all that remains of wickedness (left foot)

3. in humility receive the word implanted, which is able to save your souls (right foot)

Those three points correspond to the theme of the anger of man vs. the righteousness of God. Man's anger = bad, and bad = sin. God's righteousness = good because God is the Judge of all things and he says it is good (cf., verses 2-20). Man and his anger = the left foot, while God and His righteousness = the right foot.

The Greek word translated "filthiness" in verse 21 (*ruparia*) fits in the Biblical Greek category *hapax legomena* ("things spoken only once"). This Greek word appears only this once in the New Testament. It refers to dirt and things which make a person dirty. In verse 21 it is used figuratively for moral defilement.

The Greek word translated "wickedness" in verse 21 is *kakia*. Two words in the Greek New Testament are translated "wickedness" or "evil" (i.e., "bad"). These are,

- *kakia* (the root and vine of evil)
- *poneria* (the fruit which grows out of *kakia*)

Verse 21 doesn't employ *poneria* but *kakia*, and this is significant, brothers and sisters. It is commonplace for believers to be taught how to be a "Christian" by following certain rules and regulations. The criteria to be followed = stop sinning and start living as Jesus lived (i.e., righteousness).

Here's the thing about that. It isn't a valid method of spiritual child rearing. It amounts to picking the fruit of sin (aka *poneria*) off the tree of the sin nature in the believer. Trouble is, that sin nature goes right on growing more *poneria* day after day.

This approach is even used to get unbelievers saved. Believers condemn them for this, that, and the other evil things traditionally found on a list of "sins", and they are exhorted to stop doing them—else God won't like them. Oh, so if they pick enough fruit off the *kakia* sin tree, then God will like them, even while the *kakia* sin tree keeps on growing and bearing more fruit of sin?

Egads! What sort of evangelism is that?! First they need to be saved. This entails cutting down the *kakia* sin tree, not picking the *poneria* fruit off the tree. Only then can they be expected to cease bearing anymore *poneria* fruit of sin.

What does this have to do with verse 21, you wonder? Yes, you do. I heard you wonder with my own two ears. It's like this. Verse 21 doesn't exhort the believer to "put away" (or "lay aside") the fruit of evil (*poneria*). What good is that? The evil tree (*kakia*) simply keeps growing more evil fruit (*poneria*)!

No, but verse 21 exhorts the believer to lay aside the evil tree itself (*kakia*). That is how to get rid of the evil fruit which continuously grows on the evil tree.

The Apostle Paul phrases this as putting off the old man (the sinner) and putting on the new man (Christ in us, the hope of glory; cf., Ephesians 4:22-24). The believer is able to do this because he has died, and his life is now hidden with Christ in God (cf., Colossians 3:1-3). His evil tree (*kakia*) has been cut down.

The Greek word translated "humility" is *prautes*. The Biblical concept of "humility" is often misunderstood. It's seen as being like Caspar Milquetoast, or Wimpy of Popeye cartoon fame.

That is not the Biblical concept, brothers and sisters! Biblical humility is best seen as "gentle strength". Teddy Roosevelt's expression fits well with Biblical "humility". As U.S. President he explained his foreign policy thusly: *Speak softly and carry a big stick!* Speak softly = "gentle", and a big stick = "strength".

To practice "humility" requires the believer to *receive the word implanted*. It alone *is able to save his soul* (verse 21).

What we have been explaining corresponds with *the word implanted*. The Greek word translated "implanted" is *emphutos*, from *em* (in) + *phuo* (to plant) = "to plant in".

Oh, my aching head! What does it all mean, teacher? Just this, O distressed saint. A sinner is saved by grace through faith. God offers it free of charge to the sinner. That is God's <u>grace</u>. The sinner receives God's saving grace "by faith".

Biblical faith = believing what God says in His Word. This belief must begin in the head (i.e., understanding it); but it must also be copied by the Holy Spirit and pasted into the sinner's heart, thus creating new life. If God's Word only grows in the head, then it is intellectual "faith", not the new life of the Holy Spirit in him.

Pastor James is writing to Jewish <u>believers</u> in the *diaspora* (i.e., the Gentile lands). Believers are already saved. Ergo, they believed the Word of God already and so they are born again. Hence the Word of God is <u>already</u> <u>planted</u> <u>in</u> both their head and their heart. That is what Pastor James refers to as *the word implanted*.

For a believer to practice humility ("gentle strength") requires that he walk in the Spirit and not the flesh. Walking in the flesh = doing what he thinks is right in his own eyes, which also = doing it in his own power. That is when *the anger of man* suddenly flares up.

This is where Pastor James is coming from. The believer must first put aside *kakia* (the evil tree, the sin nature; verse 21[a]). Only then can he receive the word implanted, much less do so in "humility". The emphasis, you see, is on "humility"—"humility" comes first in verse 21[b], making it the emphasis. This emphasis serves to warn the believer about walking in the flesh, which breeds sinful pride.

And as we all know full well, sinful pride is the polar opposite of Biblical humility.

This highlights a pattern, a set of steps the believer is to take. He begins with Biblical humility, or gentle strength which he has because of the Word of God and the Holy Spirit in him. God is both strong and gentle simultaneously.

The next step after humility is the Word of God which is planted in him as a believer.

And that serves as a splendid segue to the third step. He maintains cognizance that this implanted word is capable of saving his soul.

Does this confuse you? If he is already a believer, then isn't he saved? And if he is already saved, doesn't that mean he already has received the implanted word? How, then, can Pastor James tell him to receive this word, when he already did receive it?

It's like this. In freshman algebra class the teacher tells the students to receive algebra. A wise freshman raises her hand and responds that she already had algebra in middle school. Does the teacher send her to the office to receive a different math class?

Uh, not so much. The freshman already did receive beginning algebra class in middle school, but she still needs to receive more advanced algebra classes in high school…and college too! By the same token, the believer receives God's Word in order to be saved, but that is only the start of his new life. He must continuously receive God's Word throughout his walk on earth, in order to continuously mature spiritually into the image of Jesus.

The initial reception of God's Word, so as to be saved, is known in theology textbooks as *justification*. The continuous reception of His Word thereafter goes by the nomenclature *sanctification*. The third aspect of God's salvation for sinners is *glorification*, which occurs at the Rapture when believers receive their spiritual bodies of eternity. The <u>three</u> aspects together are <u>one</u> eternal salvation, but in terms of time and space they follow the following progression,

1. justification: declared not guilty when born again
2. sanctification: spiritually maturing throughout life
3. glorification: receive a spiritual body and enter eternity

Now let's apply this to verse 21 of our text for today. To whom is Pastor James speaking? Answer: Jewish <u>believers</u> who live in the *diaspora* (the Gentile lands). Hence they are already born again. Therefore, *justification* (Aspect #1) isn't the issue.

Well, then, is the Rapture occurring? Are these believers entering eternity in their spiritual bodies at that moment? Uh, not so much.

The process of elimination leaves us with Aspect #2: sanctification as the **context** for verse 21. Pastor James doesn't exhort Jewish believers to be born again, nor to get themselves up in the clouds, bedecked in their spiritual bodies, and meet Jesus there to return with Him to heaven.

No, indeed! Brother James exhorts them to *receive the implanted word*, for the purpose of spiritually maturing into the image of Jesus. As they do so—as they grow the Word of God which was planted in them at rebirth—it will save their souls.

How so? Answer: not by being born again, that's for sure! We just went over that issue. It's called Aspect #1 of God's salvation, remember? The issue in verse 21 is spiritually maturing after rebirth. They are already saved. They're already born again!

But for believers to truly <u>know</u> they are born again, they need to see the fruit of being born again. The seed of new life (aka rebirth) was <u>planted</u> <u>in</u> them at rebirth. If they are the good soil of Jesus' parable, then the seed of God's Word will bear the fruit of God's Word, which is *putting aside all filthiness and all that remains of wickedness,* and *in humility receive the word implanted* (verse 21).

Beware the teachings of some believers. In theology textbooks they wear the name *Arminians.* These brethren teach that believers can—and many actually do—lose their salvation. By extension they teach that, though a believer is saved by grace through faith, he must do good works (the fruit of salvation) in order to stay saved.

They think they spot these doctrinal teachings in their Bible, as for example verse 21 of today's text. They fall on their faces though, when they fail to distinguish the three aspects of salvation while interpreting the text. We don't make these three aspects up. They appear with regularity in the New Testament. Let's list a Biblical text with each aspect for you to read and muse upon:

1. justification (Romans 5:1)
2. sanctification (Philippians 2:12-13)
3. glorification (1 Thessalonians 4:16-17; 1 Corinthians 15:44, 51-52)

We expound on these text at length in our books. You may wish to study them with us. All of our books are available at our online bookstore: https://randyg555.wixsite.com/heavenly-citizens/shop. For the above Bible verses you will want *Romans: Volume 9, Philippians: Volume 16, Thessalonians: Volume 18, 1 Corinthians: Volume 12* of our *Heavenly Citizens* series.

God never tells us in His Word to decide if someone is truly born again or not. That is the prerogative of King Jesus. He will judge every person based on this issue. Those who are not born again will be judged at the Great White Throne after the Millennium on earth (cf., Revelation 20:7-15). They will be found guilty of not having received Messiah Jesus as their sin offering, and therefore are still in their sins. The verdict will be "Guilty!", and they will be sentenced to the lake of fire eternally.

Those who are truly born again will not be judged as to whether or not they are truly saved. They are truly born again, after all! All true believers will be judged at the *Bema*, which is the judgment seat of Christ for believers (cf., 2 Corinthians 5:10).

The purpose of this event is to judge how much each believer "served Jesus" on earth after his rebirth. The judgment will take into account the ministry King Jesus assigned him, the spiritual gifts the Holy Spirit gave him to perform the ministry Jesus assigned him, and how well he did from the heart what Jesus assigned him to do (cf., 1 Corinthians 3:10-15).

With that being said, let us now press onward in the text:

> *But prove yourselves doers of the word, and not merely hearers who delude themselves* (verse 22).

Whenever you hear someone quote a verse from Scripture, using it to "prove" that a doctrine is true, be sure to apply Rule #1 for Bible study to the verse. This approach will test whether their claims about the verse actually are true. Rule #1 teaches,

> *A text without a context is a pretext.*

One way to apply this rule is to keep it in the **context** of <u>what precedes</u> it. In the case of verse 21, for instance, we interpreted it based on what Pastor James said in verses 2-20. And that we did. Now, so as to confirm that our interpretation is accurate, we should test our conclusions by <u>what follows</u> it in the text. Let's do this now, as we vet verse 22.

Verse 21 concluded with, *In humility receive the word implanted, which is able to save your souls*. Use plain-speak, Pastor James! How specifically are we to do that? Answer:

> *But prove yourselves doers of the word, and not merely hearers who delude themselves* (verse 22).

Take a gander again at verse 21. Focus on the clause, *the word implanted, which is able to save your souls*. How is the implanted Word of God to save the believers' souls? Answer: by them being *doers of the word, and not merely hearers*.

In other words true believers have their hearts transformed by the implanted Word of God which they received at rebirth. Because their heart is changed by the Word of God, they put it into practice in their life (i.e., they become *doers of the word*).

Many a person hears the Word of God, is convicted of his sins, and calls on Jesus to save him. Yet he either doesn't go further than that, or he behaves churchy for a brief spell before returning to life as usual pre-rebirth. Behold! the rocky soil of Jesus parable (cf. Matthew 13:3-6; 20-21).

Such a person has been changed only emotionally. The emotions wore off and he stopped being "changed" (or lost his salvation) because he was never truly changed in the first place. He was *merely a hearer who deluded himself* (verse 22 of today's text).

And then there is the person who… Oops! We let time escape us. Now we have to pay for our lack of discipline, by waiting for the morrow to learn about the next guy.

But not to fret! We will get to him first thing in our next study. For now get yourself to the prayer closet and enjoy a visit with Jesus. He wants to more fully explain what we learned today.

James 1:22-25

Jesus' *Parable of the Soils*. We were immersed in that fine spiritual teaching, when we ran out of time yesterday. So let's get right back to it, and savor the flavor of the spiritual truth which seasons every word of this parable.

We are musing on this parable in the context of verses 21-22 of today's text. Our *Arminian* brethren think suchlike texts "prove" that believers can, and do, lose their salvation. We are spending considerable time on these verses to validate or invalidate their doctrinal position.

Jesus' *Parable of the Soils* speaks directly to this issue. Indeed, Jesus explains it with crystal clarity, so that even a child can learn the spiritual truths involved. Four soils are presented, each soil representing a type of person, as he will be judged by his response to the Word of God when he hears it.

The first type of soil (or person) isn't applicable to verses 21-22 of today's text. Pastor James writes to Jewish believers in the *diaspora*, if you recall. The first type of soil (the beaten path) hears the Word of God and it has no effect whatsoever on him. Ergo, he doesn't even claim to believe it, so he cannot be included with the Jewish <u>believers</u> to whom Brother James writes.

The other three types of soil do represent folks who have an affirmative response to God's Word when they hear it. We finished vetting the second type of soil (the soil on rocky ground) in our last study. So we won't speak further of it, except to note that we are vetting the parable sparingly, only in terms of how it applies to verses 21-22 of today's text.

Feel free to study this parable with us in *Matthew: Volume 7* of our *Heavenly Citizens* series, where we go into it in much more depth.

The third type of soil (or person) hears the Word of God, also is convicted of his sins, and calls on Jesus to save him. He behaves churchy <u>for an extended, even indefinite, period of time</u>, and may even enjoy studying God's Word—though his propensity is more often than not to prefer man's books about God's Book, rather than feed on God's Book itself.

And yet his heart never becomes changed by it. Voilà! the thorny soil of Jesus' parable (cf. Matthew 13:3, 7, 22). Such a one was changed only intellectually. Intellect doesn't per se wear off for quite some time, if at all; so a person who is thorny soil may well spend his lifetime in the church building, thinking he is saved because of it.

If this type of person falls away from Jesus (i.e., he stops being "changed"), it also is because he was never changed in the first place. He wasn't saved and lost his salvation. He was *merely a hearer who deluded himself* (verse 22 of today's text).

This brings us to the fourth and final type of soil in Jesus' parable, about a person who hear God's plan of salvation for sinners by grace through faith, apart from any works of the Law or man's laws. Jesus names him the good soil. Listen to Jesus portray him:

> *And others (seeds—R.G.) fell on the <u>good soil</u> and yielded*
> *a crop, some a hundredfold, some sixty, and some thirty*
> [Matthew 13:8; emphasis ours—R.G.].

Did you spot the difference between the "good soil" and the other three types of soil in Jesus' parable? No, it has nothing to do with going to church or keeping busy "serving Jesus". We are to notice that none of the other soils *yielded a crop*.

That is the difference between born again folks and those who only think they are born again. Soil #1 had no interest in God's Word.

Soil #2 concealed a heart of rock just below it, so God's Word was unable to penetrate it and *yield a crop*. Soil #3 grew a plethora of weeds. Have you ever heard the maxim about mixing oil and water? Well, weeds and crops don't mix either! Ergo, thorny soil is also unable to *yield a crop*.

Soil #4 alone represents a truly born again person. He can be <u>seen</u> as being born again by the fact that he grows spiritual fruit in his life (cf., Matthew 13:3, 8, 23). But beware! Plants require time before crops begin to grow on them. With humans, the time required is often much longer before this occurs.

So don't go about inspecting everyone in your church to <u>see</u> if they have fruit, and then judge them accordingly. A specific type of fruit determines if a person is truly born again, viz., <u>spiritual</u> fruit; and it isn't visible to the naked eye. This is why only Jesus can judge any person as to his spiritual condition.

Even more, the seed which landed on thorny soil did grow plants. The trouble was that the plants were choked out by the weeds which fill this type of soil. Some weeds look almost identical to the wheat (or other plants which are farmed). Folks in the church building <u>see</u> these weeds and think, "What truly born again people they are! Looky there at all the fruit!" Again, only Jesus can judge any person as to his spiritual condition.

The moral of the story is that no mere man can <u>see</u> if a person is truly born again or not. Jesus is our Judge, not any mere man. He sees the heart: we don't, not even our own. He is an expert at discerning counterfeit fruit: mere man not so much. Each believer is called by God to examine his own heart and judge self, so he won't have to be judged by Judge Jesus in eternity.

When a believer examines his own heart, then, what is he to look for in making a diagnosis. Answer: only Jesus can truly judge any person's heart. This includes a believer, as he examines his own heart. The examination is spiritual, and as we keep emphasizing,

> *Nothing spiritual ever transpires apart from [1] the Word of God and [2] the Holy Spirit.*

Is the believer taught God's Word by the Spirit daily? A believer is to examine his heart by sitting alone with Jesus, with his Bible open and man's books closed, and his hands folded in prayer. While there, the believer is to begin by confessing his sins to Jesus and repenting of them. This means he turns back from sin to righteousness "in Christ". And he asks for the Holy Spirit to fill his heart and mind, and teach him the Word of God about his heart.

After he is spiritually cleansed in this manner, the believer then prays for wisdom in discerning the ministry which King Jesus assigns him to do for Him, and the spiritual gift(s) which the Holy Spirit gives him for doing this ministry. Both the ministry and the gifts are spiritual, so they aren't the natural gifts with which he was born. He didn't receive his spiritual gifts until he was born again.

The spiritual fruit of the believer—and only a believer can bear spiritual fruit because unbelievers are not spiritual—but spiritual fruit comes from the believer, as he performs the ministry King Jesus assigns him. It must be done in the power of the Holy Spirit, not in the power of the flesh. And it requires the believer to employ the spiritual gift(s) which he received from the Spirit at rebirth.

Reread the italicized words four paragraphs prior. Pay special attention to the numerals 1 and 2 there. Do you see how the italicized paragraph teaches in condensed form what took us the prior three paragraphs to explicate? It is imperative that every believer feed himself on the Word of God each day, and that this feeding be done by the Holy Spirit. Like an infant in his highchair, we must allow the Spirit to feed us (cf., 1 Corinthians 2:10-16).

In order to be sure we don't skip any spiritual meals each day, let each of us be sure to,

> *Establish a spiritual regimen of daily quiet time alone with Jesus, Bible open and man's books closed, with hands folded in prayer.*

Back to verse 22 of our text for today. Pastor James phrases the act of *yielding a crop* (as per Jesus' parable) as *prove yourselves doers of the word, and not hearers only.* This identifies the fruit which grows in the believer who is good soil: it consists of <u>both</u> hearing God's Word for him personally <u>and</u> then <u>doing</u> it (i.e., putting God's personal Word for him into practice, or obeying it).

Now take this application back to the prayer closet, where we were just moments earlier. There we were, meeting with Jesus, each of us alone, and praying for Him to examine our heart. We want Him to reveal to us what should remain in our life, and what should go, not so we can "know" facts but so we can,

> *...put aside all filthiness and all that remains of wickedness, (and) in humility receive the word implanted* (verse 21).

See! If we study the Bible in the manner we demonstrate in our *Heavenly Citizens* series, we learn the spiritual truths which Jesus wants us to know. And these spiritual truths are confirmed to us by what follows each one of them in the text of Scripture.

Consider, for example, our Arminian brethren, and their manmade doctrine about a believer losing his salvation. Does any **context** in Pastor James' letter specifically address this issue? No, we are not asking if verses 21-22 teach this issue, but is that issue a specific purpose of this letter. Stick with the context, brothers and sisters, and avoid falling in the ditch of manmade doctrines.

We cannot overstate the spiritual truth we are studying at this juncture of the text, brothers and sisters. Stop at this time, turn in your Bible to Matthew 7:15-27, and read! All of the teachings which Messiah Jesus taught in Matthew 5-7, which goes by the moniker *Sermon on the Mount*, is summed up in those final words of Matthew 7.

In verse 22 of today's text Pastor James warns the church folk lest they *delude themselves*. Messiah Jesus phrases it as taking the broad road, when only the narrow road leads to heaven (cf., Matthew 7:13-14)—in other words those on the broad road have *deluded themselves*. Jeremiah the prophet warns how the heart of man is deceitful and desperately wicked, so who can understand it (cf., Jeremiah 17:9)—in other words those who follow their heart *delude themselves*.

No amount of "serving Jesus" can ever replace <u>both</u> hearing His Word <u>and</u> being doers of what we hear. The issue isn't *justification* (becoming saved and/or staying saved). The issue is *sanctification* (living as already saved, yet not so as to remain saved, but to be who we already are).

> *For if anyone is a hearer of the word and not a doer, he is like a man who looks at his natural face in a mirror; for once he has looked at himself and gone away, he has immediately forgotten what kind of person he was* (verses 23-24).

Messiah Jesus is superb at speaking to the common person. Pastor James learned how to imitate Jesus in this. He employs a humorous simile to illustrate the spiritual truth just taught in verse 22, about not just hearing God's Word but also doing what we hear.

Imagine you are getting ready for church one fine Sunday morn. You are at the bathroom mirror, and you finish shaving. The wife and kids have already hied off to the church building because they have to get something ready, so you are on your own this morning. They can't point out anything you might have overlooked and prevent embarrassment.

Having finished shaving, you rush to the bedroom and don your Sunday best, put on your shoes, and make a mad dash for the car. With no one home to rush you, dad, you are running late. Anyway, you get to the church building and walk in. Everyone turns and mysteriously gapes at you. You enter the sanctuary and find wife and kids and sit down by them.

Lo and behold, but wifey looks aghast at you, while the kids hide their face in their hands, embarrassed to be your kids! Why would they do that, you wonder? Stop wondering, sir. You can be sure wifey will tell you…

Turns out you still have shaving cream under your chin, and a few drops of blood on your neck which is smeared on your shirt collar. Don't you feel the dufus, sir? You should. You looked at your face in the mirror, then instead of fixing the mess, turned around and walked away, leaving the mess for all to see.

That is one potential scenario which Pastor James had in mind, as he penned verses 23-24. Let's be sure to keep the **context** of these verses in mind, as we vet them. This section of the text began with verse 19, where Brother James warned believers that they *must be quick to hear*. You recall that, don't you? Waddaya mean no? Then reread the verse!

You will also (hopefully) recall that James did <u>not</u> say, *Be quick to hear, then turn around and forget what you heard!* No, but he said, *Be quick to hear, slow to speak and slow to anger*. That is how verses 22-24 fit into this section of the text. Believers are to be quick to <u>hear</u>, yes, but then be just as quick to <u>do</u> what they hear.

In verse 24 the original Greek text is quite precise in its tenses. We speak of the verbs translated "gone away" and "he was". The first Greek verb is perfect tense, the second imperfect tense. Now don't go working yourself up into a lather. You might forget about the shaving cream under your chin and the drops of blood on your neck and shirt collar. We're going to explain these verb tenses to you in plain-speak.

The Greek perfect tense identifies an action which occurred only one time in the past, but the effects of the action still continue on into the present. In the case of verse 24, "gone away" = he looked in the mirror at his face, then he "went away and stayed away" from the mirror. The scenario Pastor James presents in verses 22-24 is that of the Word of God being the mirror, to show man his <u>spiritual</u> condition.

Applying the perfect tense to a hearer who doesn't also do what he hears in God's Word, we learn that such a one sees his spiritual condition in God's Word when he hears it in a sermon; but then he walks away without correcting what he sees as wrong in his life. Even more, being perfect tense, after he walks away, he stays away! He doesn't allow God's Word to bring the issue up to him anymore. Yikes! He makes himself permanently impenitent!

Oh, there was another Greek verb to add to this spiritual quagmire. Remember the Greek imperfect tense verb we mentioned three paragraphs prior, the one translated "he was"? Yes, that one. Well, the imperfect tense refers to an action of the past which was continuously done. This contrasts with the perfect tense thusly:

- perfect tense = one-time past act, its effects still continue
- imperfect tense = continuous past act

Now let's apply this to our <u>hearer</u> who doesn't also <u>do</u> what he hears in God's Word. He "went away and stayed away" from

God's Word (the mirror). In doing so he forgot what God's Word revealed to him, what he needed to correct to be right with God. The imperfect tense "he was" tells us "he continuously was" this way in the past. It was the person "he was" and saw in the mirror.

Pastor James employed three short verses to teach a spiritual truth, where Messiah Jesus was wont to present the same spiritual truth in the form of a lengthy parable. We pointed you to Matthew 7:15-27 a bit earlier in this study as an example of this.

Both Jesus and James presented a common occurrence in today's church building. Some folks go to church, sit in a pew, stand up and sing a hymn, sit down and hear a sermon, and learn to say "Amen" at the end of a prayer. When the church service is over, they exit the church building and get back to "real life"—which is defined as what it is they live for the rest of the week. Once outside the church building, like the rocky soil they immediately forget everything they heard until the next church service. Oh, and they continue that way until the next church service too.

That is the scenario with which Messiah Jesus concludes His *Sermon on the Mount* (Matthew 7:15-27). Pastor James paints a more concise scenario of the same scene in verses 22-25 of today's text. Is the Bible relevant for us today? If you think not, we are sorry to have to tell you, but you have failed to heed Jesus' parable and James' mini-parable.

> *But one who looks intently at the perfect law, the law of liberty, and abides by it, not having become a forgetful hearer but an effectual doer, this man will be blessed in what he does* (verse 25).

Verses 22-24 presented the parable of a person who goes to church and hears the Word of God, but then immediately forgets what he heard and gets back to the "real world". Verse 25 then brings into the parable the person who hears the Word of God, but instead of immediately forgetting what he heard, he puts it into practice in his daily living in the "real world". Jesus did the same in his parable at the end of the *Sermon on the Mount.*

The Greek word translated "looks intently" is chock-full of visual imagery. The word is used five times in the New Testament: 1x right here by James, 1x by Peter, and 3x in the Gospel accounts of the empty tomb.

The Apostle Peter explains that the Old Testament prophets did not serve themselves but God's people in the Church. They didn't get to know the full meaning of all the revelations about the Messiah, of whom they prophesied in Scripture. Then Brother Peter adds, *Things into which angels long to look* (cf., 1 Peter 1:12). "To look" is the same Greek word that James uses ("looks intently").

Doctor Luke uses this Greek word to describe what the Apostle Peter did, after he heard the women's account of what occurred when they went to Jesus' tomb on resurrection morning. Luke records how Peter hied off to the tomb as fast as his feet would take him. When he got there, *stooping and looking in, he saw the linen wrappings only* (cf., Luke 24:12).

The Apostle John employed the same Greek word twice. The first occurrence was the same event which Doctor Luke recorded, about Peter at the empty tomb (cf., John 20:5). The second occurrence was about Mary at the empty tomb. She did the same thing Peter did (cf., John 20:11).

Do you see the significance of this Greek word? Out of the five times it is employed in the entire New Testament, three of those occurrences reveal the actions of Peter and Mary at the empty tomb. They "stooped down and looked in". How much do you think they wanted to see Jesus? That is how **intense** this word is.

James 1:25

Yesterday we began our trek through verse 25. The verse is integrally connected to verses 19-24. The specific "trial" (or "test" or "temptation") of this section of the text has to do with being *quick to listen and slow to speak.*

The **context** for those two instructions is the third instruction: being *slow to anger.* To fail to listen, but instead to have a propensity to spout off the first feelings to be aroused in us, cannot but lead to anger. Anger is the fruit of this, and the listen/speak dichotomy is the root and vine which grows the fruit of anger.

Those who have control over their tongue tend to be those who are not regularly angry. Contrariwise, those whose tongues wag freely are hotheads. Their anger is worn on their sleeves.

Before delving further into verse 25, let's press F5 to refresh our memory of the verse. Or we can simply reread the verse…

> *But one who looks intently at the perfect law, the law of liberty, and abides by it, not having become a forgetful hearer but an effectual doer, this man will be blessed in what he does* (verse 25).

Verse 22 exhorts the believer to not just <u>hear</u> the Word of God, but to also <u>do</u> what he learns from hearing the Word of God. Verses 23-24 then address a believer who only <u>hears</u> God's Word. Verse 25 follows this up with a synopsis of a believer who both <u>hears</u> and <u>does</u> the Word of God.

Our last study concluded with an analysis of the Greek word which is translated "looks intently". It is used of the Apostle Peter and Mary, when they went to Jesus' tomb to see His body. They were too late. Jesus already rose out of death!

But they didn't know this yet. So when they arrived at the tomb, they stooped down to look inside. The imagery has to do with them making every effort it took to get to that tomb, and then to see the body of Jesus. They didn't simply amble along Cemetery Lane on a sunny spring morning, getting their cardio workout for the day.

No! They purposefully poured themselves into getting to Jesus' tomb and gazing upon His body. Mary did so because her broken heart wanted to see Him again. Peter did so because the ladies of the church shocked him by saying His body was no longer there. But in both cases they were <u>driven</u> to see Jesus' body. They were impelled by their heart to see Him. That is the **intensity** of this Greek word, brothers and sisters.

In verses 22-25 Pastor James distinguishes the rocky soil believer from the good soil believer. The rocky soil cannot grow the Gospel seed. Why? Because the seed tries to grow, but it dies of thirst. How come? Because the soil is a thin layer sitting on top of rock. The seed needs to put out roots deep into the soil, in order to drink the moisture below. The rock below the surface of the soil prevents that from happening; so the seed dies of thirst (or hibernates).

The rock signifies a person's heart, which is hardened by worldly matters. He is so distracted by them, so preoccupied with them, that those worldly matters petrify him. Oh, he can still hear the Word of God. In fact he is distinguished from the beaten path soil, in that the Gospel seed doesn't remain atop the soil. It does enter the soil and briefly seem to grow…before it dies of thirst!

As Jesus explains such a one, he "believes" momentarily only, which itself signifies that only his emotions are excited by this new thing he hears. Such is the hearer-only of Pastor James' mini-parable. His supposed "salvation" is only emotional. But as we are well aware, emotions are up one moment, down the next.

Then comes verse 25. The believer of this verse not only <u>hears</u> the Word of God, but he responds by <u>doing</u> what he hears from the Word of God. This begins with the Greek word into which we just delved. He not only <u>hears</u> God's Word, but also <u>does</u> God's Word. Doing God's Word requires a believer to *look intently into it*.

The "it" is phrased in verse 25 as *the perfect law of liberty*. That is a depiction of the Word of God. The Apostle Paul is on the same page as Pastor James. Small wonder, seeing how the Holy Spirit inspired the both of them to write Scripture.

In 2 Corinthians 3 Brother Paul addresses the issue of many of Jewish folks not being able to hear the Gospel and respond to it correctly. This was because they had a veil over their heart. Hence when Moses was read (i.e., *Torah*, or the Law of Moses), they failed to hear the spiritual truth which portrayed Messiah Jesus.

Brother Paul then holds out Biblical hope to them, saying that by turning to the Lord Jesus, the veil over their hearts (which blocks out spiritual truth) is taken away. Then follows this:

> *Now the Lord is the Spirit, and where the Spirit of the Lord is, there is liberty* [2 Corinthians 3:17].

The contrast is stark as all get-out. On one hand are those who hear the Bible, who in Paul's case above are those who hear "Moses". They are hearers who don't also do what they hear by turning to the Lord. On the other hand are those who "turn to the Lord", which identifies believers. They both <u>hear</u> and <u>do</u>.

Then comes the crux of the matter, as it pertains to Paul and James being on the same page, viz., verse 17 of 2 Corinthians 3 as quoted above. True believers have "liberty", the same Greek word which Pastor James uses in our text for today. Oh, and if you continue reading in 2 Corinthians 3, the next verse teaches,

But we all, with unveiled face, beholding as in a mirror the glory of the Lord, are being transformed into the same image from glory to glory, just as from the Lord, the Spirit [2 Corinthians 3:18].

Why, looky there, ma! Believers are known for looking intently in a mirror, yes, even the mirror of God's Word. As they do so, they become transformed into the image of Jesus. Pastor James sees the Word of God as a mirror, as does Brother Paul. James teaches the need to "gaze intently" into God's Word, as does Paul (verse 13). James teaches that those who do so have liberty "in Christ", as does Paul.

Funny thing that, how all of Scripture fits together, as if only one Person wrote all of it in one sitting as one "novel". Can better evidence exist of how all of Scripture is divinely inspired by one and the same Person, the Holy Spirit (cf., 2 Timothy 3:16-17)?

But why is God's Word given the moniker *the perfect law, the law of liberty* (verse 25)? It's like this. Every son of Adam the First is conceived in sin and born in iniquity (cf., Psalm 51:5), which makes all of us sinners.

It is a fact of life that we cannot make chicken salad out of chicken feathers. Sinners sin. They don't live righteously. Therefore, when push comes to shove, sinners are unable to choose correctly between sinning vs. righteous living. In plain-speak, sinners have no choice (no "liberty"). They must sin. It's in their genes.

But when a sinner is born again as a saint, we just learned from the Apostle Paul what happens to him. The veil which blocks spiritual truth in God's Word is removed from his heart. He is able to <u>both</u> see spiritual truth as he hears God's Word <u>and</u> do what he sees. He can make a choice between sinning vs. righteous living. The Spirit in him empowers him to obey…but only if he chooses to do so.

God never forces anyone to be saved, and He never forces any saved person to live as being saved. Christian living is the walk of faith. Faith comes from hearing the Word of Christ (cf., Romans 10:17). It is up to the believer to continuously choose to <u>hear</u> God's Word, and then to continuously put it into practice in his daily living (i.e., to <u>do</u> God's Word).

That, brothers and sisters, is the definition of the Greek word translated "looks intently". The believer must *look intently at the perfect law of liberty*, if he is to spiritually mature into the image of Jesus and so live like it.

Casual glances at a verse or phrase in the Bible won't cut it. Substituting man's words about God's Word won't cut it. And reading the daily newspaper, and books about pursuing worldly pleasure, certainly won't cut it! There is no such critter as *Buffet Bible*. We can't pick and choose the spiritual dishes we want to eat.

To "look intently" into the Word of God means to stoop down low and look into the empty tomb, to see for self that Jesus is truly risen. He is! And the sinner is by faith to first die "in Christ" on the cross; then he is by faith to rise out of death "in Christ" to newness of life. This newness of life means that the veil over our heart is removed, and we are capable of understanding spiritual truth in God's Word.

It is up to you, O believer. Do you want to spend the rest of your life on earth, feeding on the Word of God daily so that you become transformed into the image of Jesus? Or are the world and the things of the world tying you down to the ground?

We believers are in earthly shoes, yes, with our feet on the ground; but we are heavenly citizens who look upward for our daily living. We are free to choose righteous living, but we can choose sinful living instead. Living <u>for</u> the world = sinful living. Living <u>in</u> the world for Jesus = righteous living. Choose you this day whom you will serve. But as for me and my house, we will serve the Lord Jesus and enjoy His "liberty" (cf., Joshua 24:15).

By the way, the original Greek text of verse 25 translates as,

But the one who stooped down so as to look into the perfect law of liberty… (verse 25 literal).

This is why we have been quoting it that way, rather than as the NASB translates it. The NIV translates it thusly:

But whoever looks intently into the perfect law that gives freedom [James 1:25; NIV].

King Jamie thought to translate it in this manner:

But whoso looketh into the perfect law of liberty [James 1:25; KJV].

What follows in verse 25 is Step #2 of Pastor James' instruction for Christian living. Step #1 = the believer "looks intently" into the Word of God (which spiritually matures the believer so he has the "liberty" to choose righteous living over sinful living).

Step #2 is that the believer *abides by it*, which means he continues looking intently into God's Word. He remains in the Word daily.

A caveat comes on the heel of Step #2. Let not the hearer become distracted by the world. Neither let him become so busy "serving Jesus", that he hasn't time to spend alone with Jesus to feed on the Word of God daily (cf., verse 25^c).

The result of verse 25$^{a\text{-}c}$ follows in the remainder of verse 25:

…this man will be blessed in what he does (verse 25^d).

(The reader is encouraged to look intently into Psalm 1 now.)

The concept of "blessed" is that a believer receives God's favor. God prospers him because the person aligns himself with God's will for his life. This doesn't entail rushing hither and yon through the church building, like a chicken with its head cut off, as he is busy "serving Jesus"! It consists of,

> *Establishing a spiritual regimen of daily quiet time alone with Jesus, Bible open and man's books closed, with hands folded in prayer.*

That is the only way of life which will bring true "blessing", true spiritual life, to any of us. There are no shortcuts. It is a way of life, life itself. It is a "He", the "He" being Jesus the Messiah, the God-Man. We know of no more blessed life than being alone with Jesus, where we are remade into His image.

First a person must <u>be</u> a new creation "in Christ". He must become alive spiritually (aka *justification*). Second, he must <u>live</u> the new life instead of the old life. This is a lifetime process by which he spiritually matures (aka *sanctification*). It is not possible to live spiritually without first being spiritual (i.e., being born again).

The Greek word translated "liberty" means "freedom", as in being free from slavery. Every son of Adam the First is born a slave to sin. Sinful man by definition cannot but rebel against the authority of God over His creation. We won't have this Man Jesus to reign over us! We will sit on the throne and rule!

The only path to true "liberty" (or "freedom") comes from looking intently into *the perfect law of liberty*, which is God's Word, the Gospel of Jesus Christ. This "law" is "perfect" because it is the only means by which sinful man can be "perfected". Spiritually speaking, to be "perfected" = becoming "complete", so that each of us is as God intends for him to be. The more a believer spiritually matures into the image of Jesus, the more perfect, the more perfected, he is. God's Word alone can accomplish this in man. God's Word is the "perfect law" because it perfectly saves.

As this process of spiritually maturing progresses in a believer, he ceases to be "a forgetful hearer". Increasingly, he metamorphoses into "an effectual doer". He not only hears and then <u>does</u>, but he does what God instructs him to do in His Word "effectually". The original Greek text reads,

> ....*he has become not a forgetful hearer but a doer of work* (verse 25[c] literal).

The entire **context** of this section of the text has to do with only hearing God's Word vs. hearing God's Word and then doing what it says. Ergo, the phrase "a doer of work" means that the "work" done comes from God's Word.

A believer who continues to feed on God's Word daily while alone with Jesus, and then puts into practice what the Holy Spirit teaches him, becomes increasingly perfected (aka spiritually mature). Such a one *will be blessed in what he does*. The blessing is future tense, and this future blessing is twofold:

1. blessed in heaven at the *Bema* (the believer's reward)
2. blessed in his earthly life (to see his life bear fruit in others)

For more on the believer's rewards at the *Bema*, we invite you to study *Revelation: Volume 11* with us. It is available at our online bookstore: https://randyg555.wixsite.com/heavenly-citizens/shop.

James 1:26-27

Hearers vs. hearers who then do what they hear. We have spent considerable time on this topic, haven't we? It began with verse 19, and it doesn't end until verse 27 (the end of chapter 1).

In our last study we finished vetting verse 25. Without further ado, we will rush right into the clover field of verse 26.

> *If anyone thinks himself to be religious, and yet does not bridle his tongue but deceives his own heart, this man's religion is worthless* (verse 26).

Do you see how verse 26 connects with what precedes it in the text? Waddaya mean no? Look harder! Focus on the clause,

> *...and yet does not bridle his tongue but deceives his own heart* (verse 26^b).

Now reread verse 19. Do you see it now? Don't tell me you can't see it. Waddaya mean you still don't see it? As the famous secret agent Maxwell Smart was fond of phrasing the matter, "I asked you not to tell me that!" Verse 19 reads,

> *But everyone must be quick to hear, slow to speak and slow to anger* (verse 19^b).

Verse 26^b is the polar opposite of that! Instead of listening ("be quick to hear"), the person of verse 26^b has no bridle on his tongue, which is the opposite of "slow to speak". A bridle goes in the horse's mouth, and serves to direct the horse where it is to go (like the steering wheel of a car).

Pastor James puts the finger on anyone who supposes himself to be "religious" (i.e., a good ol' boy in the church building). Brother

James tells him that, should his tongue control him rather than he control his tongue, then his basket of religion is empty!

Imagine it like Little Red Riding Hood, as she is off to see the wizard, er, we mean to see Grandmama. In her hand is a basket full of goodies for granny to eat. Well, she arrives at granny's house and enters, then heads to granny's bedroom to find granny in the bed…only it's not granny but the big bad wolf. But Little Red doesn't know this…incredibly.

But we digress. Little Red hands the basket full of goodies to granny, who looks inside and finds it empty. So she, er, we mean it eats Little Red instead! That's Pastor James' version of the tale.

So it is for the Big Bad Wolves in the church building. They would be those who think themselves so "religious". They come to every service, stand up at the right time to sing, sit down and bow the head at the right time to pray, and add a touch of "Hallelujahs" and "Amens" on occasion to make the service more "spiritual".

And yet the proverbial flies on the wall of their houses, which see them 24/7/365 behind closed doors, never observe them opening their Bibles. Nor are they seen on their knees conversing with King Jesus. By all appearances, when they are alone and have no one to pat them on the back and anoint their heads with accolades for being super saints—at such alone times as these their "religion" is quite indiscernible from anything most every unbeliever practices.

When it comes to these Big Bad Wolves in the church building, Pastor James excoriates their showy performances as "worthless". The Greek adjective means "empty" or "vain". It serves no good purpose.

The Greek adjective translated "religious" in verse 26 occurs only this one time in the entire New Testament (i.e., a *hapax legomenon*, or a word spoken only one time). It is a safe bet that Pastor James, being the Hebrew he was, interpreted "religion" in terms of *Torah* observance as it was done by the Pharisees.

Anyway, such a state of affairs was offensive as all get-out to Brother James. He censures all believers who think to continue this outward showmanship, which is devoid of any inward reality. It amounts to having spiritual fruit without first having a spiritual tree to grow the fruit! As Jesus phrased it, it is a whitewashed tomb, empty graves with a pretty façade.

A believer in the church building who is all show and no blow *deceives his heart*. Do you see it? His "religion" is deceptive because his very heart is deceived. His outward show manages to fool a lot of other folks in the church building. He is so good at it, that he deserves an Oscar for his performance!

The more fully an actor can identify with the character he plays, the more realistic is his performance. Seeing how this believer in the church building has deceived his heart, small wonder his religious performance is so effective. But in the end this religious show is "worthless". It is useless. It accomplishes no good purpose. You may fool the people, but you cannot fool Judge God.

The Greek noun translated "religion" is the noun form of the Greek adjective translated "religious". However, unlike the adjective, the noun doesn't occur only once in the New Testament. The noun occurs four times, twice in James, once in Colossians, and once in Acts. The other occurrence in James is in the next verse (verse 27).

In Colossians 2:18 this noun appears in the phrase, *self-abasement and the <u>worship</u> of the angels*. The noun "worship" is this Greek word. The Apostle Paul employs it in portraying the manmade religion known as Gnosticism. This religion teaches the secrets for how man can make himself right with God. Ergo, the Greek word translated "worship" in Colossians (or "religion" in James) has to do with outward behaviors without any true spiritual root and vine.

In Acts 26 the Apostle Paul is testifying to King Agrippa about his life. He first portrays his early years, how he was brought up. Let's listen in on his riveting account:

> *...I lived as a Pharisee according to the strictest sect of our religion* [Acts 26:5].

The religious sect to which Brother Paul made reference was the Pharisees. They were the one whom we addressed above, whom Jesus verbally flayed for being whitewashed tombs, empty bones on the inside with pretty religious paint on the outside. Ergo, in this case also the Greek noun translated "religion" has to do with lots of outward fleshy appearance but no inward spiritual substance.

Conclusion: based on all four of the New Testament occurrences of the Greek word *threskeia* ("religion"), the noun has to do with outward religious behaviors and practices, with no corresponding inward spiritual life to grow true spiritual fruit.

With this understanding fresh in our gray matter, let us now proceed to the next and final verse of chapter 1.

> *Pure and undefiled religion in the sight of our God and Father is this: to visit orphans and widows in their distress, and to keep oneself unstained by the world* (verse 27).

The word translated "religion" appears in both verse 26 and verse 27, with the difference being that it is in its adjectival form ("religious") in verse 26 but a noun in verse 27. These two verses are joined at the hip by this Greek word (*threskeia*). Our job is to get a handle on what this word means in the **context** of this text.

In prior paragraphs we learned that, in James' letter, the concept of "religion" does not denote the religious practices of the Gentiles, in contrast to Jewish worship which is based on God's Word. Not at all. Believers learned straightway that Jewish worship at the temple and synagogues = rabbinical interpretations of *Tanakh* (aka the Old Testament), substituted for *Tanakh* (God's Word) itself.

Today believers are inclined to do the same thing. This is evident when Christian leaders are held up as the authorities over what the Bible teaches. Some examples are dependence on,

- doctrinal statements instead of the Bible
- Sunday School booklets instead of the Bible
- a favorite author who we respect instead of the Bible
- famous evangelists or TV preachers instead of the Bible

Take careful note of how, in each example, the Bible is relegated to the back burner, while some super saint is elevated to the front. Such an approach to knowing God's Word exalts man's words in some form over the Bible, good intentions notwithstanding.

Listen up, O believers! The Bible is not too hard for you to read and comprehend. God doesn't make mistakes. He didn't give us His Word in an incomprehensible form to many of the believers, so that they have to go to a priest to explain it to them.

God went to great pains to give us His Word, and spent millennia preserving it for us, so that we can relate to Him personally. Why would anyone in his right mind want to know about God via man's words (aka head knowledge alone), when he can go to God directly via His Word and the Holy Spirit, and actually know God personally? Sin makes us crazy, brothers and sisters, wicked crazy.

Religion = man's words of any kind as a substitute for God's Word. False religions in the world ignore the Bible in favor of their own "holy books". Cults pretend to choose the Bible, but in practice have their own "holy books" which interpret the Bible; and their interpretations are the only correct understanding of the Bible. Alas, but their interpretations go counter to the Bible on many levels, especially on the level of who Jesus is (His Person) and what He does (His Ministry).

In complete and total contrast to "religion" is the Gospel. The Gospel is life itself, eternal life. It is available from God alone, and without money and without cost (i.e., "grace"; cf., Isaiah 55:1). It is received by Biblical "faith". Faith comes from hearing the Word of Christ (cf., Romans 10:17).

The Gospel is heard, and the hearer believes it in his head, followed by the Holy Spirit copying it and then pasting it in the hearer's heart. In James' words, be both hearers and doers!

What does all this have to do with verse 27? Just this. Verse 26 depicts "religion", man's words instead of God's Word, as the instructions for how to relate to God. A religious person may well "hear" God's Word, but he doesn't "do" what it says. Instead, he resorts to man's words to explain God's Word to him, and follows those interpretations. The result = "religion", following man rather than following God…and all of them fall into the ditch together!

Oh, but Pastor James doesn't leave us in the ditch. He follows verse 26 with verse 27, in which "pure and undefiled religion" is set in stark contrast to all forms of man's "religion".

First note that "pure and undefiled religion" is defined as being acceptable *in the sight of our God and Father*. On the other hand, any and every form of man's "religion" is categorically not!

Secondly—and this is crucial to recognize because it reveals the Jewish approach to life—but Pastor James contrasts the fruit which grows out of man's "religions" with the fruit which grows out of God's religion. This is the Oriental thought process at work. It stands in stark contrast to the Occidental mode of reasoning, which clings to Aristotle as our rabbi.

The Oriental mode of reasoning emphasizes the <u>fruit</u> of our life, the Occidental emphasizes the <u>root</u> <u>and</u> <u>vine</u> which grows the fruit. Both approaches include both the root/vine and the fruit, but the emphasis is what distinguishes them from each other. Consider the specifics of this in verses 26-27:

- *does not bridle his tongue* (man's religion)
- to visit orphans and widows in their distress, and to keep oneself unstained by the world (God's religion)

Here's the thing about the Oriental approach. Pastor James doesn't say, "If you want to get to heaven, visit orphans and widows in their distress, and keep yourself unstained by the world." Even Orientals realize that fruit needs a tree or vine on which to grow, with the root and vine being the true life which bears the fruit.

In other words, Brother James isn't teaching how to be saved (*justification*). He is teaching how to live as saved (*sanctification*). It is the height of folly to think James practiced Pharisaism in the Church! James followed Jesus, not the Pharisees.

The Pharisees were all about their outward appearance, i.e., being fashionably religious. That wasn't enough to please God. Messiah Jesus—and James was His disciple—but Jesus taught that a tree is known by its fruit (cf., Matthew 7:15-23). So a person is not right with God by his fruit (i.e., his behaviors and works); rather, if he is right with God, then his fruit will also be acceptable to God.

The bottom line is this, brothers and sisters. A true believer will spiritually mature into the image of Jesus. This will show itself not simply by him being in the church building, and talking Bible words and slogans learned from man's books; nor from the busy-bee syndrome of works, works, and more works, without time alone with Jesus each day, as He feeds the believer His Word and involves the believer in His life with Him personally.

In verses 26-27 Pastor James gives a couple of examples of the works of "religion" vs. the works of new life (see our list six paragraphs prior). Those are only examples. The specific <u>fruit</u> a specific believer is to produce depends on the specific ministry King Jesus assigns him to do for Him.

But produce spiritual fruit every believer will, if he is a true believer. True believers have spiritual hearts and minds. Such a spiritual tree/vine cannot but grow spiritual fruit. God isn't sterile! Hence those who have God living inside them (i.e., believers) are not sterile either!

The Greek word translated "orphans" is *orphanos*. You can see our English word in the Greek word. Simply delete the Greek suffix "os", and voilà! our English word "orphan". The Greek word means the same thing as our English word, viz., having no father and mother.

This tells us our English word is a *transliteration* rather than a *translation*. A *translation* replaces the Greek word with an English word which means the same thing. A *transliteration* keeps the Greek word and changes the Greek letters to English letters which sound the same. Let's illustrate a *transliteration*:

- ὀρφανός
- orphan

This Greek word appears in the New Testament only twice, here in James and also in John 14:18, where, on the night preceding His crucifixion, Jesus encouraged His disciples with the words, *I will not leave you as orphans*.

The Greek word translated "widows", on the other hand, occurs twenty-seven times in the New Testament. Most of these are in the Gospels and 1 Timothy, with 1 Corinthians having one occurrence and Acts having three.

The point of import for the words "orphans and widows", as they are used by Pastor James here, is that the phrase harkens back to what has come to be known in today's Church as the *Deacon's Fund*. The early Church helped to care for widows and orphans of believers (cf., Acts 4:32-37). As Pastor of the Jerusalem Church, Brother James most certainly had this practice in mind, when he penned verse 27 as an example of the fruit of a believer. Paul also taught the Gentile believers to support the Deacon's Fund.

But the Deacon's Fund wasn't the only fruit of a true believer which James noted in verse 27. The other fruit was that the true believer *keep himself unstained by the world*. In verse 26 the fruit of an unbeliever only has one example. In verse 27 the fruit of a true believer receives two examples. The two go together as two peas in a pod. The two together, you see, identify both sides of the same coin, the coin being the true believer.

The first example of spiritual fruit in verse 27 (visiting widows and orphans) = doing good to believers in need. The second example comes from the opposite direction, to teach believers what not to do, or what must be avoided at all cost. Fruit #1 = what to do, Fruit #2 = what not to do. This is the same approach King Yahveh employed in *Torah* (aka the Law of Moses) to teach the Israelites. The commands fell into two categories:

- do this
- don't do that

The phrase *keep oneself unstained by the world* is one of countless examples throughout Scripture which teach the *Doctrine of Separation*. God is holy, so anyone who will have a relationship with God must also be holy (cf., Leviticus 11:44; 1 Peter 1:16). The phrase James employs in verse 27 conjures visions of the words used by Jude in Jude 1:22-23.

A New Testament example of this for the Church—aside from James and Peter and Jude as noted in the prior paragraph—is to be found in 2 Corinthians 6:14-18. Read it. You will be shocked by how serious God is, when it comes to His kids keeping apart from the devil's kids.

In the **context** of James' letter to the Jewish believers in the *diaspora* (i.e., the Gentile lands), those in the Church who bear worldly fruit overall, without any spiritual fruit, are to be treated as unbelievers. Such folks need to repent and live spiritually, if they would be a part of the spiritual Family of God (cf., 1 Corinthians 5). With that let us retire to the prayer closet and meditate at the feet of Jesus on these many Bible passages.